Praise for the first edition

" A clear, practical book that explains the nature of crowdsourcing and shows how to apply it in your business.

David Alan Grier, First Vice President, IEEE Computer Society and Associate Professor of International Science and Technology Policy, George Washington University

" Businesses harnessing crowdsourcing are infinitely more successful than those that don't. The question is — what should a business do and where should they start? Ross is THE guru to answer these questions sharing his wealth of experience in a concise and engaging way in his latest book.

Maria Sipka, CEO, Linqia

Getting stuff done has forever changed thanks to the internet and online access to skills. This book makes sense of the crowdsourcing trend for BOTH buyers and providers of services. My favorite section is that ethics, integrity and good citizenry must still underpin all actions. Relationships and reputation matter more than ever in a connected and transparent world; this guide is invaluable to business people who want to transform the way they resource projects.

Annalie Killian, Director of Innovation and Social Business, AMP

" If you want to leverage the talent of a crowd - and why you wouldn't you? — this is the ultimate guide. It gives you insight into how to best use it to your advantage and fly with your powerful idea.

Luca Penati, Global Managing Director, Ogilvy PR

" Getting Results From Crowds is one of those books where you're mad at the authors... for not writing it sooner. Getting Results from Crowds sells itself as a guidebook where you can dip into the different piece of the material as you have the needs.

Prof. Terri L. Griffith, Author of The PLUGGED-IN Manager

" This book is a crowdsourcing bible for companies or individuals that can be applied to almost any industry on the planet.

Epirot L. Nekaj, Founder of Ludvik+Partners

> " Ross Dawson and Steve Bynghall have masterfully delivered a comprehensive and strategically pragmatic guide to crowdsourcing. Each chapter elegantly lays out a key concept and then provides practical advice. This is the must read bible for effective crowdsourcing. "
>
> **R "Ray" Wang**, Principal Analyst & CEO, Constellation Research

> " To many business executives crowdsourcing is a mysterious concept and they struggle to understand what it is, when to apply it and how to go about it. Ross's latest book is a fantastic guide for businesses looking to access skills and drive innovation through crowdsourcing. I highly recommend it. "
>
> **Peter Williams**, CEO, Deloitte Digital

> " Ross Dawson, the "crowd king", provides with Getting Results from Crowds a comprehensive and up to date review of how to make crowds work for you! "
>
> **Matt Barrie**, CEO, Freelancer.com

> " To make the most of the different crowdsourcing options available for your business grab a copy of 'Getting Results from Crowds' — it will pay for itself many times over! "
>
> **Mark Harbottle**, Founder, 99designs.com

> " Once again Ross has nailed a complex topic and made this appealing to business executives striving to make sense of crowd-sourcing. He clearly explains how business can grow more effectively from the social connecting power of free forming (opt in) networks. As always, Ross's books are jam packed with real stories of pioneers not only changing the world of work as we know it, but also he helps to inform and guide our leadership practices. A must read if you are serious about the changes underway and want to compete more effectively to harness simply the intelligence of everyone. "
>
> **Dr. Cindy Gordon**, CEO Helix Commerce International Inc, and Co-Founder SalesChoice Inc. & Author of Business Goes Virtual, Why Buy The Cow, Collaboration Commerce: The Next Competitive Advantage, Realizing the Promise of Corporate Portals

> " This is the smartest, most practical overview of crowdsourcing I've seen (and I think I've seen them all). It will be particularly valuable in helping larger and more established companies to adopt crowdsourcing. "
>
> **Lukas Biewald**, CEO, CrowdFlower

Getting Results From Crowds

Second edition

October 2012

For Daniela, a pleasure to meet! Ross Dawson

Authors: Ross Dawson and Steve Bynghall

Senior researcher: Jackson Carroll

Researcher: Claudia Pelzer

Designer: Daniil Alexandrov

Advanced Human Technologies

San Francisco · Sydney ·

About Advanced Human Technologies

Advanced Human Technologies is a leading international consulting, content, and ventures firm.

Consulting: We help companies create exceptional business value in the network economy.
Publishing: We publish high-value content and develop thought leadership content for clients.
Ventures: We establish new ventures in content, online, and mobile.

For more on Advanced Human Technologies' services see:
www.ahtgroup.com

About the authors

Ross Dawson

Ross Dawson is globally recognized as a leading futurist, entrepreneur, keynote speaker, strategy advisor, and bestselling author. He is Founding Chairman of three companies: Advanced Human Technologies, future think-tank Future Exploration Network, and events company The Insight Exchange. His books include the Amazon.com bestseller *Developing Knowledge-Based Client Relationships* and the prescient *Living Networks*. He has delivered keynote speeches on six continents, with clients including many of the largest companies in the world. Ross frequently appears in the world's leading business media.

For more on Ross Dawson's keynote speaking and strategy advisory work see:
www.rossdawson.com

Steve Bynghall

Steve Bynghall is a London-based freelance consultant and writer specializing in enterprise collaboration, knowledge management and intranet themes. Steve worked in a professional services environment for twenty years in a variety of knowledge-related roles, including managing the global extranet program at accounting firm BDO. In 2010 he set up his own company, Two Hives Ltd. As well as client work, Steve has carried out various projects for the Intranet Benchmarking Forum (IBF) and writes the report for the annual Intranet Innovation Awards, organised by Step Two designs. Steve has also written the text for several movie tie-in books aimed at children for Dorling Kindersley.

ISBN 978-0-9847838-2-3

Table of contents

How to read this book

You do NOT need to read this book from front to back or beginning to end. Dip into it however you find useful

Feel free to skim through it until you find something you want to spend more time on.

This is a guidebook: Use it when needed to design and implement projects that draw on crowds.

Each chapter is intended to provide practical guidelines, illustrated by a case study.

Part I provides a useful introduction if you are new to the concepts of crowds and crowdsourcing.

We'd love to get your feedback, particularly on how we can make the second edition even better! Go to **www.resultsfromcrowds.com** to share your thoughts.

Introduction

We are connected. That changes many things from the world of yesteryear, including how we find information, socialize, research purchases, and even find spouses. However one of biggest impacts of connectivity is on the world of work.

As value in the global economy shifts inexorably towards knowledge and deep expertise, an ever-increasing proportion of work transcends location. From individual tasks through to complex team-based projects, most work can be done anywhere on the planet.

This is a boon to organizations of all kinds, which can find and tap the most relevant talent wherever it resides. In particular, for entrepreneurs this is the dawning of an age in which the power of the idea reigns supreme. There is today a capacity unparalleled in human history to bring sophisticated ideas to life at a limited cost. Moreover, the ability to fund ventures from many financial contributors is creating extraordinary new possibilities.

On the other side of the market, talented people with specialist expertise can access clients and markets not just locally but all around the world. This provides opportunities for individuals and the communities around them that simply did not exist a scant few years ago.

On top of the simple fact of connected work, the last decade has seen the creation of a variety of mechanisms to aggregate and distil talent, insights, and even capital. Service marketplaces give access to talent, competition platforms uncover the best creative concepts, crowdfunding taps contributions from fans, and idea management tools help identify and build on relevant suggestions.

'Crowdsourcing' is the term most often used to describe these approaches, though we prefer the more general concept of tapping the power of crowds.

There is no question that accessing the talent of crowds provides immense potential for organizations to be more efficient, become more competitive, and grow faster. However that doesn't mean it is easy to do, or do well.

A significant proportion of organizations that try service marketplaces or other crowdsourcing tools do not have good experiences, and many do not return to try them again. That's usually because they have gone about it the wrong way, and with inappropriate expectations.

This book is designed to be as practical and useful as possible, helping individuals, entrepreneurs, and organizations to get the most from crowds through the use of dedicated tools, platforms, and approaches. Developing these skills will become a critical competence for almost all organizations.

This book's primary audience is the clients of crowdsourcing and crowds and those building business models based on crowds. However we have also included a chapter for service providers, as this is an important crowd business model. In addition, to build valuable business relationships with providers, there is little more useful than gaining a deeper understanding of their issues and concerns.

We have used several crowd approaches in creating this book. However to get valuable input it is often useful to provide something concrete that people can improve on. As such, the second edition of this book will draw far more on broad participation. We'd love to get your input on how to improve this book at **www.resultsfromcrowds.com**, where you can join the broader discussion on how best to get extraordinary results from crowds.

We wish you all success in your journey of tapping the potential of crowdsourcing.

Ross Dawson
Steve Bynghall

Acknowledgements

We would like to thank those who kindly gave their time and shared their expertise in interviews for the book or allowed us to reproduce what they have written: Davy Adams, Matt Barrie, Tracey Corcoran, Stef Gonzaga, Ron Holifield, Philip Letts, Jerry Macnamara, Casey McConnell, Nick McMenemy, Kim Murgatroyd, Mike O'Hagan, François Petavy, Avnesh Ratnanesan, Yannig Roth, Mike Sampson, Fabio Rosati, Sakin Shrestha, Sarah Sturtevant, Gary Swart, Mike Todasco, John Winsor, and Elizabeth Yin. Thank you!

PART I

FUNDAMENTALS OF CROWDS

1 Crowds and crowdsourcing

2 The rise of crowdsourcing

3 Crowds and business value

4 When to use crowds

CROWD BUSINESS MODELS — VIII

USING OTHER PLATFORMS — VII

CROWDFUNDING — VI

MANAGING PROJECTS — V

USING SERVICE MARKETPLACES — IV

BUILDING RELATIONSHIPS — III

APPLICATIONS OF CROWDSOURCING — II

FUNDAMENTALS OF CROWDS

Crowds and crowdsourcing

> " *Thanks to the Web... companies that move now can leverage a global pool of talent, ideas, and innovations that vastly exceeds what they could ever hope to marshal internally.* "
>
> **Kevin Maney**, Technology Editor, USA Today

We have entered a new era in which organizations are able to tap the extraordinary power of crowds of people located all over the planet. The introduction of the term 'crowdsourcing' has been valuable in helping to communicate and popularize these ideas.

Chapter overview

- The term 'crowdsourcing', introduced in 2006, describes how the contributions of many can create value.

- Service marketplaces that match clients and providers of services are not crowdsourcing in the strictest sense, but are a key way in which crowds create value.

- Related concepts include on-demand workforce, mass collaboration, open source, and open innovation.

- Our crowdsourcing landscape identifies 22 categories of platforms and tools that help tap the power of crowds.

The power of crowds

The power of the crowd is here. The use of crowds to support innovation and business ventures is hardly a new phenomenon. However a number of trends over the last decade, not least pervasive low-cost communication technologies, mean that the use of crowds has become a fundamental enabler of work and business.

In the first instance, literally an entire world of workers, many of them extremely talented, are now available to companies. This is transformative on a number of levels. It means anyone can draw on some of the most talented people in the world, if they can provide them with interesting and rewarding challenges. It also means that startups can tap a diverse array of relevant skills from the outset, even before having sufficient funds to hire full-time staff.

In addition, the world of Web 2.0 has generated tools that can create valuable, emergent outcomes from mass participation. We now have the structures and platforms that can make the idea of the 'wisdom of crowds' into a reality. Technologies built on principles of emergence are bringing to life the long-held dream of collective intelligence.

In short, we are rapidly shifting into a world in which:

THE POWER OF IDEAS REIGNS SUPREME

Today ideas can be proposed, identified, realized, and scaled far more effectively than ever before. We are entering a new era of business.

Understanding crowds and crowdsourcing

The term crowdsourcing, coined by journalist and author Jeff Howe in 2006, has helped us to frame the concept of using crowds to get work done. Implicit in the idea of crowdsourcing is the ability to create value that transcends individual contributions, crystallizing collective insights through structured aggregation.

For example competitions, prediction markets, idea filtering, and content rating are all mechanisms by which collective contributions can create better outcomes than individuals or small groups.

However it remains true that accessing the talent of the most relevant individuals within a large crowd is one of the best ways to create value, given the global access we now have.

In this report we use the term service marketplaces to describe platforms such as oDesk, Elance, and Freelancer.com, that connect clients with the most relevant individual workers or small teams.

In the strictest sense of the word these are not crowdsourcing tools, as they are marketplaces where buyers and sellers can meet rather than aggregating the contributions of many to provide a collective outcome. However they are still an important – and arguably the most important – way in which crowds are creating value for business today.

In this book we use both the terms 'crowds' and 'crowdsourcing'. Our core theme is how businesses can get results from using crowds, including the mechanisms of crowdsourcing.

Definitions of crowdsourcing

"Tapping the minds of many."

– Ross Dawson

"Crowdsourcing is the act of taking a job traditionally performed by a designated agent (usually an employee) and outsourcing it to an undefined, generally large group of people in the form of an open call."

– Jeff Howe
(The White Paper Version)

"The application of Open Source principles to fields outside of software."

– Jeff Howe
(The Soundbyte Version)

"Crowdsourcing is a neologistic compound of Crowd and Outsourcing for the act of taking tasks traditionally performed by an employee or contractor, and outsourcing them to a group of people or community, through an "open call" to a large group of people (a crowd) asking for contributions."

– Wikipedia

"A business model or function that relies on a large group of users as third parties for outsourcing certain tasks. The popular use of the internet makes communication and coordination progressively cheap: tasks that would have been impossible to communicate and coordinate before have become extremely easy to set up and coordinate."

– Financial Times Lexicon

Related concepts

On-demand workforce
Also sometimes described as "labor-as-a service" or "cloud labor", this refers to tapping workers to deliver services as required. This is usually implemented through service marketplaces, as described in detail in Section III of this book.

Collective intelligence
This age-old idea has been brought into focus by the tools of connection and collaboration we have built over the last two decades. It perhaps aspires to a more pure view of human potential than the more commercially-oriented purview of crowdsourcing.

Mass collaboration
This is closely aligned to the concept of crowdsourcing, in describing how many working together can create value. The term is useful for encompassing the full scope of how these mechanisms of participation are relevant across business, society, and government.

Co-creation
Co-creation (closely related to "peer production") describes generally how value is created by groups, usually referring to work across organizational boundaries or between companies and their customers. Some forms of co-creation, notably obtaining input from many customers, are effectively crowdsourcing.

Web 2.0
The essence of Web 2.0 is in creating collective value from mass participation, using web-based tools to aggregate activities and contribution in useful ways. As such many aspects of Web 2.0 are in essence crowdsourcing. The term is now less frequently used as 'social media' has come into vogue to describe many aspects of Web 2.0.

Open source
Open source software is a powerful example of crowdsourcing, bringing together many individual contributors to create a valuable product. Key concepts of open source are being applied in a range of crowdsourced ventures, notably philanthropic product development.

Open innovation
Open innovation generally refers to how larger organizations draw on broad pools of external contributors to innovate and develop new products. This is essentially a type of crowdsourcing, and many open innovation platforms and tools are often referred to as representative examples of crowdsourcing.

The crowdsourcing landscape

There are a wide variety of different crowdsourcing models. The latest version of our Crowdsourcing Landscape identifies 22 categories of crowdsourcing tools, as shown below and on the following page. For more details and examples of each category please go to this book's companion website, **www.resultsfromcrowds.com**.

The 22 categories can be clustered into 7 types of crowd business models plus non-profit ventures. These are discussed in detail in Chapter 25 on Crowd Business Models.

Types of crowdsourcing

CROWDSOURCING CATEGORY	DESCRIPTION
Service marketplaces	Matching buyers and sellers of services.
Competition markets	Competitions awarding prizes to selected entries.
Crowdfunding	Donating to creative ventures, sometimes as a pre-sale.
Equity crowdfunding	Equity funding from many small investors.
Microtasks	Markets for very small well-defined tasks.
Innovation prizes	Prizes for single, defined innovation outcomes.
Innovation markets	Matching clients and researchers for innovation.
Crowd platforms	Software used to support crowdsourcing processes.
Idea management	Processes to propose, rank, and improve on ideas.
Prediction markets	Coalescing diverse views into collective forecasts.
Knowledge sharing	Sharing knowledge, experience, and insights.
Data	Gathering or refining data in specific domains.
Content	Creating media content.
Content markets	Enabling creators to sell their content.
Crowd design	Product design, selection, development, and marketing.
Crowd process	Aggregation and added value to marketplaces.
Labor pools	Access to groups of specialists.
Managed crowds	Aggregated services provided by selected specialists.
Crowd ventures	Businesses conceived and managed by crowds.
Citizen engagement	Contribution to civic or government initiatives.
Contribution	Philanthropic fundraising and ventures.
Science	Contribution to scientific endeavors.

Crowdsourcing landscape

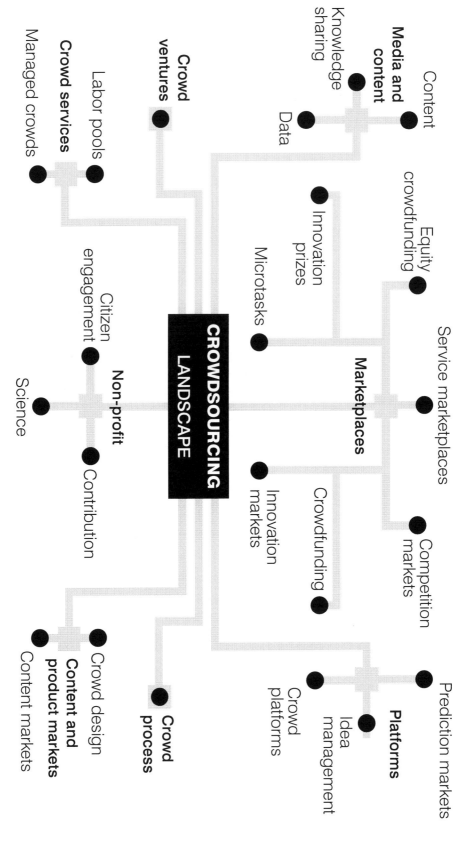

Content
Knowledge sharing
Media and content
Data

Crowd **ventures**

Equity crowdfunding
Marketplaces
Innovation prizes
Microtasks

Service marketplaces
Competition markets
Innovation markets
Crowdfunding

Prediction markets
Platforms
Idea management
Crowd platforms

Managed crowds
Crowd services
Labor pools

Citizen engagement
Non-profit
Science
Contribution

CROWDSOURCING LANDSCAPE

Content markets
Content and product markets
Crowd design

Crowd **process**

For a more detailed view of the landscape including examples of each category see the book website: **www.resultsfromcrowds.com**

The rise of crowdsourcing

2

> *Profound changes in the nature of technology, demographics, and the global economy are giving rise to powerful new models of production based on community, collaboration, and self-organization...*
> **Don Tapscott** and **Anthony D. Williams**, co-authors, Wikinomics

While the practice of crowdsourcing is not new, a variety of factors, notably the rise of digital connectivity everywhere in the world, has contributed to an explosion in the use of crowds and crowdsourcing by organizations. The underlying trends supporting the rise of crowdsourcing are well established, suggesting we are relatively early in a transformation in the practice of global work.

Chapter overview

- Crowdsourcing has a long history, with one well-known early example the British Government's creation a Longitude Prize in 1714.

- The pace of development of the use of crowds accelerated from the late 1990s, with Elance an early crowdsourcing platform established in 1999.

- Trends that are driving the rise of crowdsourcing include connectivity, collaboration tools, awareness of crowdsourcing, comfort with remote work, and efficiency pressures on organizations.

Crowdsourcing timeline

The British Government offers a "Longitude Prize" of £20,000 for a reliable method of calculating a ship's longitude

The publication of the third "Lonely Planet" Travel Guide ushers in an era of user contributed updates, tips and corrections from independent travellers

King Louis XVI of France offers a prize for producing alkali from sea salt, with Nicholas Leblanc taking the prize eight years later

The Hollywood Stock Exchange founded to buy and sell prediction shares of movies, actors, directors, and film-related options

First publication of a fascicle of the Oxford English Directory (OED), which used around 800 volunteer readers in cataloguing words

| 1714 | 1783 | 1884 | 1916 | 1957 | 1979 | 1981 | 1996 | 1997 | 1998 | 1999 |

Planters Peanuts holds contest to develop its logo

Rock band Marillion raises $60,000 from fans on the Internet to fund their U.S. tour

Jørn Utzon selected as winner for design competition for Sydney Opera House

The Rise of the E-Lance Economy by Thomas Malone and Robert J Laubacher published in Harvard Business Review

Tim and Nina Zagat establish the Zagat restaurant guide, initially drawing on reviews from their friends, and then the broader community

Elance launches as first major online service marketplace, inspired by the 1998 HBR article

XIIIV | **XIX** | **XX**

oDesk commences as a service marketplace, soon launching its Team software which monitors workers to log work performed

U.S. Department of Defense launches Policy Analysis Market for event prediction but is quickly closed after criticism of it as a "terrorism futures market"

GetAFreelancer launched in Sweden, later moved to Australia and renamed Freelancer.com

The book *The Wisdom of Crowds* by James Surowiecki popularizes the idea of the value of "collective wisdom"

Amazon.com launches the microtask platform "Mechanical Turk", which was originally developed internally to identify duplicate product pages

Design competition platform 99designs raises $35 million in its first external fund raising

Iceland government crowdsources the process for its new constitution

2000　2001　2003　2004　2005　2006　2008　2009　2011　2012

Wikipedia launches, initially as a "feeder" to the more structured Nupedia

InnoCentive set up by Eli Lilly to act as a broker between a "crowd" of registered users and the outsourced R&D requests from pharmaceutical companies

Incoming Procter & Gamble CEO A.G. Lafley announces plan to generate 50% of R&D from outside the company

JustGiving established as Internet-based platform to help people raise money for charities

ArtistShare launches as general creative "fan-funding" platform

US JOBS Act signed to enable equity crowdfunding

The Guardian crowdsources examination of MP expenses

Crowdfunding platform IndieGoGo launched

Investment into oDesk brings its total funding to $29 million

Journalist Jeff Howe coins the phrase "Crowdsourcing" in an article for Wired Magazine

Sellaband launches crowdfunding platform for music

XXI

11

Enablers of the rise of crowds

The rise of crowds and crowdsourcing over the last decade has been dramatic. While crowdsourcing is not entirely new, the rise of the Internet has provided a platform for it to become a truly global phenomenon that is transforming business. There are a variety of enablers that have supported and will continue to drive the rise of crowdsourcing.

Connectivity

The bandwidth available to individuals and organizations for a given cost has risen exponentially for the last two decades. In developed countries broadband access has become pervasive. Access to the Internet in developing countries has become easy and low-cost.

New collaboration tools

Complementing connectivity has been the development of a wide range of collaboration tools that facilitate remote work. In addition to basic enablers such as free voice and video calls, a variety of online services including project management, shared desktops, and collaborative design tools are making it easier to work remotely.

Development of crowdsourcing platforms

The continued evolution of crowdsourcing services has provided increasingly useful and solid platforms for crowd work. Innovations such as hourly billing, screen monitoring, two-way feedback, social feedback on competitions, and specialist platforms have continuously improved the crowdsourcing experience for both clients and providers.

Awareness of crowdsourcing

While it is not new, the coining of the term 'crowdsourcing', widespread media attention on the concept, and more recently well-funded advertising campaigns by prominent crowdsourcing platforms have all supported far greater visibility and understanding of the concept.

Comfort with remote work

Many managers are becoming more comfortable with the idea and practice of remote work, supported by the increase in employee telecommuting and exposure to work by remote freelancers. What seemed foreign and fraught with uncertainty is becoming standard practice.

Cost and efficiency pressures

The inexorable drive to lower costs and greater efficiencies in organizations is being driven by increased competition, easy price comparison, and new entrants from other countries and adjacent industries. All companies are continually examining their cost base and seeking ways to increase efficiency. Effective approaches to sourcing and structuring internal and external talent are recognized as critical levers for success.

Crowds and business value

3

> *Crowdsourcing is a way to import talent and creativity to your business by putting potentially thousands or tens of thousands of people to work on your problem... Learn more about crowdsourcing to see if it has applications for your business and then begin your search for solutions. It's an approach that greatly expands your business's potential.*
>
> **Lisa Gundry**, Professor of Management and Director,
> Center for Creativity & Innovation, DePaul University

In our connected world, crowd work and crowdsourcing will become increasingly central to how companies are structured and how they draw on the resources they require to do business. Executives need to understand where the greatest potential value lies for their company as well as the possible pitfalls.

Chapter overview

- The major value of using crowds for companies are to increase flexibility, access talent and ideas, reduce costs, increase capabilities, and reduce time to market.

- In assessing or making a business case for using crowds, it is important to recognize that there can be real costs and risks involved.

- The ways in which small businesses and large companies use crowdsourcing are currently quite different, but they are likely to converge over time.

The business value of using crowds

Through history, companies have been limited in what they can achieve through the scope of their internal resources and how well they can draw on external resources. Crowdsourcing has the potential to create enormous value for businesses by giving easy access to an essentially unlimited pool of talent and capabilities. Those organizations that have the skills and competences to draw on external crowds, as well as in tapping the best ideas from their 'internal crowds', have an immense advantage over those companies that rely solely on their internal resources and traditional service firms.

While there are many potential benefits of using crowds, there are five primary outcomes that create the most value for organizations.

1   **Increase flexibility**

A major benefit of using crowd work is that it is available on demand, and so is fully scalable from nothing to extremely high levels as required. Particularly for smaller organizations, this means they do not need to hire people into specific roles when they do not need a full-time person in that function, or can't anticipate their future need for that role.

This is particularly important for startups or when companies are trying new ventures that may or may not succeed. They can draw on resources as needed to establish the project. If it doesn't work, they can easily close it down, whereas if it does work, they can very quickly scale up the operations.

2   **Access talent and ideas**

Even the largest organizations in the world recognize they do not have all the talent they require internally. Drawing on crowds gives access to a vast global pool of talent, some of which will be perfectly suited to your requirements. That talent may not always be as inexpensive as some newcomers to crowdsourcing expect, but it is available to companies as never before.

One of the principles of crowdsourcing is that market mechanisms can help match needs and solutions. In distributed innovation, where companies are looking for highly specific insights and solutions, a large proportion of the winning ideas come from people who already had a good idea of the answer. The ideas you need probably already exist; now you have the mechanisms to access them.

3   **Reduce costs**

There are a variety of ways in which using crowds can reduce costs, including substituting expensive professional service firms with lower cost service providers, ensuring simple, low-level tasks are not being done by high-cost internal staff, and lowering the costs involved in innovation and product development.

In some cases these cost savings can be substantial. As noted below it is important to note that there can also be costs associated with tapping crowds. And as emphasized throughout this book, focusing solely on cost reduction is unlikely to lead to the best outcomes.

4   Increase capabilities

In many cases companies can build capabilities and undertake initiatives that simply would not have been possible without access to external crowds. For example, services that require a pool of specialists or need to be rapidly scaled can only be delivered by large companies, or those with flexible access to crowds. Microtasks enable tasks and service that simply would not have been possible previously.

In addition, crowdfunding can support a wide range of ventures that would not have been feasible through traditional fundraising mechanisms.

5   Reduce time to market

As the pressure increases on companies to bring new products and services to market faster, crowdsourcing provides valuable support in bringing to bear whatever resources are required. These can be applied to both product development work and project management functions, as well as the myriad administrative and marketing tasks that are required.

While the transaction costs of dealing with crowds limit how quickly resources can be brought in to projects, those companies with experience using crowds and established relationships can often support substantially faster project delivery.

Building a business case for using crowds

In most cases organizations will start to use crowds for specific instances, and expand from that narrow starting point once the value has become evident. As such there is usually no significant investment required, and no detailed business case is required.

However in some cases an internal business case needs to be made for new vendors to be used, and for more significant projects, for example prize-based distributed innovation initiatives or new systems that require using vendor APIs to integrate into internal business processes, sufficient investment may be involved to warrant a business case. In any case, it is usually worth carefully considering potential costs or risks as well as the possible value creation before making major shifts in business activities, even if quantification or a formal case is not needed.

A business case always needs to assess potential benefits, potential costs or risks, and also the potential cost of not taking action. In many cases, including implementing crowdsourcing, it is a mistake to focus solely on quantifiable financial costs and outcomes.

Potential costs and risks of using crowds

While there are potentially many benefits of tapping crowds in business, recognize that there are potential costs compared with other approaches, as well as risks. Below is a list of the primary potential costs and risks you should be aware of in using crowds in your business.

Costs	
	COMMENT
Learning	Building capabilities in using crowdsourcing effectively requires time and effort.
Quality assurance	Sometimes additional resources need to be allocated to checking quality of external work.
Process implementation	More sophisticated approaches where crowdsourcing platforms and approaches are integrated into existing internal business processes require work and possibly technology development.

Risks	
	COMMENT
Reduced quality	There is the potential that internal or client-facing work and projects will not meet existing standards.
Project overruns	It is easier for projects to overrun in costs or time if there is less control over the resources on the project.
Loss of intellectual property	There may be greater exposure of intellectual property to theft or loss.
Reduced staff motivation	If the adoption of crowdsourcing is mismanaged then employees could feel their contributions are not valued.
Loss of capabilities	If inappropriate functions are passed over to crowd work then core competences of the organization could erode over time.

Using pilots

In most cases it is very difficult to assess either likely benefits or potential costs of using crowds without having had any practical experience. As such, the best way to build or assess the case for using crowdsourcing is to run pilots with a limited scope, that are designed to identify and capture insights into the value for the business.

As in any pilot project, the usual issues apply of selecting the right projects to start with, involving enthusiastic people who will try to make it work, designing to achieve specific business benefits and generate useful lessons, encouraging experimentation, and creating visibility. A clear timeframe should be set after which a decision is made to cut, continue, redefine, or expand.

Using crowds in small business and big business

Over the last decade, crowdsourcing in various guises has had a substantial impact on how business is conducted across companies large and small. However current and future approaches to crowdsourcing are quite different depending on the size of the company.

More recently uptake has been significantly stronger within small organizations than larger companies. The visibility of crowdsourced services has dramatically increased over the last few years. The very obvious benefits of drawing on crowds has attracted those companies that are most easily able to change their work processes.

Small business use of crowds

Service marketplaces and competition platforms are the two types of crowdsourcing most used by small and mid-sized business. There are minimal barriers to using these services, with immediate benefits in terms of broadening access to providers and achieving competitive costs.

In smaller organizations business owners can readily drive change and adopt new ways of working, which makes the adoption of crowdsourcing easier.

Creative individuals and groups in domains such as film, music, and design usually have significant financial constraints, though also often have access to broad communities, sometimes of keen fans. This supports both crowdsourcing the creative process, as well as the use of crowdfunding, which to date has been largely of creative ventures.

Moving forward, it is likely that small and mid-sized businesses will start to use other types of crowdsourcing to a greater degree, supported by the emergence of platforms designed for that market. Microtasks and distributed innovation are both areas likely to experience strong growth in the smaller business market.

Big business use of crowds

The most prominent early examples of large companies tapping crowds has been in distributed innovation, often described as 'open innovation'. Procter & Gamble, IBM, Eli Lilly, and Boeing are some of the companies that for over a decade have been tapping large numbers of external scientists and researchers to drive their new product and innovation pipelines. These have included both internally driven initiatives such as Procter & Gamble's R&D Connect program or IBM's alphaWorks, and establishing and using open platforms such as InnoCentive.

Public competitions in which significant prizes are offered have long been part of the business landscape. Increasingly these will shift onto competition platforms to become part of a broader landscape of competitions and competitors that are used to drive business value.

Idea platforms that help to identify, filter, and action ideas from within and sometimes beyond an organization's employees have been used for well over a decade, however are gradually becoming more commonplace. Alongside these, prediction markets are well-suited to use within large companies as they need a significant minimum threshold of participation to achieve meaningful results.

Crowdsourcing aggregators, as described in Chapter 23, are often ideal for large organizations, as they usually include the associated professional services needed to design and run larger crowd tasks. More generally the use of microtasks is rapidly rising as a way to contain costs and expand capabilities in a variety of arenas.

While so far larger organizations have tended to quite specific use of crowd approaches focused on innovation, we are seeing an increasing number of big companies start to use service marketplaces to assist work processes. Moving forward, we believe many large organizations will place a high priority on creating value from internal and external crowds.

When to use crowds

4

> " There is no "in" or "out" anymore. In the hyperconnected world, there is only "good" "better" and "best," and managers and entrepreneurs everywhere now have greater access than ever to the better and best people, robots and software everywhere. "
>
> **Thomas Friedman**, Pulitzer-Prize winning journalist and author, *The World Is Flat*

The potential of using crowds continues to expand as the talent pool broadens and platforms evolve. However this doesn't mean that tapping global providers is always the best approach. Organizations need to consider when they should use crowds, and how best to go about finding the right kinds of providers for the tasks required.

Chapter overview

- Companies need to carefully consider the strategic question of what could and should be done inside and outside the organization.

- In many cases there are good reasons to draw on local rather than global providers.

- Distinguishing between when commodity or talented providers are required allows use of the most relevant approaches.

- Protection of intellectual property is a significant consideration, but risks are often over-estimated and can be mitigated.

The shifting line between inside and outside

In 1937 the then-young English economist Ronald Coase published a paper titled 'The Nature of the Firm' in which he described why organizations exist. Over five decades later, in 1991, he received the Nobel Prize in economics for his insights. Coase had pointed out that the cost of internal transactions is often lower than those for external transactions. When you go outside the firm, you have to find providers, assess offerings, develop trust, and manage the relationship. For many tasks it is more efficient to get tasks done internally than to go outside. This gives rise to large complex organizations.

As many authors of the dot-com era pointed out, in a connected world transaction costs are greatly reduced. It has become far easier to find suppliers, compare them, and build effective working relationships. The rise of crowdsourcing is one of the most important examples of this shift. Transaction costs are continuing to fall as a result of developments such as improved reputation systems.

As transaction costs fall, those organizations that do not look outside for services and talent when it makes sense to do so are at a strong competitive disadvantage. Yet there are still real reasons for organizations to exist. Certainly almost completely virtual organizations can prosper today, however there remain sometimes significant advantages to developing internal capabilities.

In considering using external talent here are three key questions to ask:

1   Inside or outside?

2   Local or global?

3   Commodity or talent?

Once the decision has been made to use external talent there are further issues to address, such as whether to pay using fixed fees or hourly rates, which will be examined in Chapter 11 on Specifying.

Inside or outside?

The first question to ask about any particular task is whether it should be performed inside or outside the organization. For most organizations, there are many functions that can readily be performed externally. They are a long way from hitting the boundaries of what can and should be done outside.

The first constraint is in the organization's preparedness to use external workers or crowds. Being ready culturally and having the processes and structures in place to crowdsource effectively (see Chapters 9 and 18) provide a foundation to begin taking work outside the organization.

Ultimately, there are a number of issues that constrain the tasks and functions that can be done externally. In particular, the increasingly pointed strategic question that senior executives and boards must address is what resides inside and outside the company. The organization's strategy must clearly answer that question, defining the company's position.

Limits to external work

	WHEN TO DO WORK INTERNALLY	COMMENTS
Regulation	If regulation restricts the external disclosure of information e.g. privacy.	In many cases if data is encrypted then work and analysis can be done externally.
Confidentiality	If information is proprietary and there are substantial risks if it is made available to competitors or others.	This is fundamentally an issue of trust. Some information is sufficiently sensitive never to share externally. Most confidential information can be shared with external providers once there is a strong enough relationship and sufficient trust. Contractual and legal remedies can help, but do not substitute for trust.
Understanding of context	If work requires a significant understanding of the context and issues surrounding the work to be performed effectively.	External providers can develop a sufficient understanding of context, however this takes time and is developed over the course of an extended relationship.
Teamwork	If work requires significant ongoing unstructured interaction within loosely defined teams.	External providers that over time have established trust and have good communication skills can perform effectively in distributed teams.
Core competence	If capabilities are central to the strategic positioning of the organization and should be continually developed.	The scope of an organization's core competences needs to be regularly reviewed.

Local or global?

Once a decision has been made to engage external talent for a particular task, that does not necessarily mean that the workers should be selected from a global pool. There can be many reasons to draw on local talent. Organizations that build a broad pool of external providers will often find that they have a significant number that are local, and that any cost differential is balanced with the greater value local providers can create.

There are few hard and fast rules, however there are a variety of factors that each support the use of local or global providers.

Factors in selecting local or global providers		
	SUPPORTS LOCAL	SUPPORTS GLOBAL
Scope of role	Varies in scope or expands over time.	Clearly defined.
Company contact	Interaction required with a wide range of people in the client organization.	Single point of contact at the client.
Team member location	Role requires interaction with several team members who are primarily in a single location.	Team members are distributed across multiple locations.
Trust levels	Heightened confidentiality issues mean provider in same country is preferred.	Confidentiality is not a vital issue, significant trust has been developed, or contracts provide sufficient protection.
Location of customers and community	Engaging with local community provides insights, connections, and value beyond the work performed.	Customers and work are global.
Strength of relationship	Strong ongoing relationships are easier to build when in the same location.	Long-term relationships are less critical.
Degree of specialization	Sufficient pool of relevant talent available locally.	Extremely specialist skills are required.

In one case I (Ross) used a service marketplace to look for a specialist software developer. The leading contenders appeared to be in Beijing and Tokyo, and I ended up selecting the Tokyo-based provider. It turned out he was actually currently based in Sydney, where I was also working, so we caught up for a coffee to discuss the project in more detail, and were able to build a far better working relationships than if he were remote. This helps to illustrate that there need not be a complete divide between local and global providers, as well as that for top providers fees are similar, irrespective of where they are based.

Commodity or talent?

When engaging external providers, significantly different approaches need to be taken depending on whether the work required is commoditized or requires talent. Many organizations that draw on external crowds fail to distinguish between these situations, with the most common outcome the inability to attract talented providers. Given that one of the most valuable aspects of tapping crowds is drawing on uniquely talented professionals, this can significantly limit the value available through the use of external providers.

Below are some of the factors that help determine whether tasks require a commodity provider (who should still receive respect) and talented providers (who often have distinct motivations and need to be dealt with differently).

Identifying type of provider		
	COMMODITY	TALENT
Task definition	Task can be clearly defined.	Task scope and process is unclear and the provider needs to help define these.
Task importance	Task is not mission critical and imperfections will not significantly impact final outcome.	Task outcome is critical to the organization or work done for its clients.
Output visibility	Outputs will not be directly visible outside the organization.	Outputs will be visible outside the organization, including by its customers.
Task redundancy	Task can be repeated by multiple providers as a check.	Outcome is unique.
Creativity required	No or minimal creativity is required.	Creativity is fundamental to the task.

Intellectual property and confidentiality

One of the most common concerns managers and entrepreneurs have when considering outsourcing work is that their intellectual property (IP) could be vulnerable. While it is a significant consideration, it is common for overblown fears to stop people from gaining the value possible through tapping crowds.

> ❝ *The dangers of life are infinite, and among them is safety.* ❞
> **Johann Wolfgang von Goethe**, 18th century poet and diplomat

Mitigating IP risk in using crowds

These are some of the actions you can take to mitigate IP risk:

- Do not provide detailed information in the public work brief, just what is sufficient to get accurate bids. Either selected bidders, or only the successful candidate, will receive the full specification.

- Require workers to sign a Non-Disclosure Agreement before commencing work.

- Start workers on non-sensitive tasks, and only once you have built trust in them, give them more critical work.

- If data is involved, encrypt it before sharing with external providers. In most cases this should be a straightforward process that does not impact any analysis.

- Divide tasks so that no single provider can see how their task relates to the overall project. Note that there can be major costs and potential problems from using this approach, so it should only be used if absolutely necessary.

A key issue is the value of stand-alone IP relative to the value of execution of those ideas. Many would-be entrepreneurs restrict the potential of their ideas and energy by being overly cautious about protecting their idea from venture capitalists, partners, marketers, developers, and others. This results in vastly reduced chances of success. Many great ideas have never got off the ground because their creators were not able to trust others.

There certainly are real considerations of protecting ideas and IP in building businesses. However there are a wide range of risks in entrepreneurial ventures, and taking calculated risk relative to potential benefit is what drives success.

A reality check on IP protection

Here are a few things to keep in mind if you are concerned about protecting your IP when using crowds.

- You are in the best position to develop your idea, or if you are not your pressing issue is finding the right partners rather than trying to execute yourself.

- Crowd workers are intent on getting paid work in the present, and are very unlikely to want to develop ideas where the payoff is uncertain and distant.

- Very few crowd workers have the capabilities to execute projects on their own behalf and are very unlikely to want to try.

- While you may have somewhat better legal protection working with local providers compared to global workers, essentially the same risks exist.

PART II

APPLICATIONS OF CROWDSOURCING

CROWD BUSINESS MODELS — VIII

USING OTHER PLATFORMS — VII

CROWDFUNDING — VI

MANAGING PROJECTS — V

USING SERVICE MARKETPLACES — IV

BUILDING RELATIONSHIPS — III

APPLICATIONS OF CROWDSOURCING — II

FUNDAMENTALS OF CROWDS — I

Crowdsourcing for enterprise and growth

5

> *The ultimate value of an internal crowdsourcing initiative will be the creation of a collaborative culture that champions fresh ideas and mirrors the community-centric nature of the Internet at large. And that will enable the organization to channel the creativity of its employees and attract the best talent of the 21st century.*
>
> **PwC report:** Harnessing the Power of Crowdsourcing

Crowdsourcing is becoming a fundamental enabler for many successful companies. However there can be major differences in the applications and success factors of crowdsourcing between large organizations and smaller growth companies. There are a range of important ways in which enterprises can complement their existing capabilities using crowds. For entrepreneurial organizations, crowdsourcing can be central to their operations and execution.

Chapter overview

- The primary applications of crowdsourcing differ substantially between large enterprise and smaller growth companies.

- The main domains for crowdsourcing in the enterprise are innovation, marketing, processes, internal crowds, and business models.

- Specific issues for successful crowdsourcing in large organizations include culture and adoption, and governance.

- The most common applications of crowdsourcing in growth companies include software development, design, online promotion, and virtual assistants.

- Distinct issues that need to be addressed in entrepreneurial organizations include defining core capabilities, and culture.

Using crowds in big business and small business

Over the last decade, crowdsourcing has had a substantial impact on how business is conducted across companies large and small. However how crowdsourcing is used differs significantly depending on the size and positioning of the company.

Over the last few years, in general smaller and growth-oriented organizations have experienced a broader uptake of the use of crowds than large organization. This has been due both to the more pointed opportunity for resource-constrained organizations to tap external capabilities, as well as the speed and ease with which smaller companies can change if their leaders understand the opportunities.

The use of crowds has the potential to significantly impact how large organizations work. For now this has tended to be focused on specific applications for crowds such as innovation and marketing. Over coming years the use of crowds could in fact transform the structure and underlying business models of more forward-looking enterprises.

In this chapter we examine the differing priorities and issues for large enterprise and smaller growth organizations.

Crowdsourcing for enterprise

Large organizations tend to have grown built on the premise that their core talent is internal, which has constrained their inclination and openness to tapping external talent. However the emergence of a highly interconnected economy over the last two decades has led many organizations to develop rich external networks and shift their attitudes to value creation.

It is certainly more challenging for large organizations to adopt crowdsourcing, given the scope of shifts to existing processes, the response from staff, and perceived risks from external engagement. However the extremely high potential value of tapping external talent means that a substantial and increasing proportion of enterprises are now engaging in a variety of ways with crowdsourcing.

There are five dominant applications for crowds in large organizations.

1   **Innovation**

The most prominent early examples of large companies tapping crowds have been in distributed innovation, often described as 'open innovation'. Procter & Gamble, IBM, Eli Lilly, and Boeing are some of the companies that for over a decade have been tapping large numbers of external scientists and researchers to drive their new product and innovation pipelines. These have included both internally driven initiatives such as Procter & Gamble's R&D Connect program or IBM's alphaWorks, and developing and using industry platforms such as Innocentive.

Public competitions in which significant prizes are offered have long been part of the business landscape. Increasingly these will shift onto competition platforms to become part of a broader landscape of competitions to drive business value.

Customer feedback and ideas to drive product development have moved to the mainstream. While the intent is often significantly one of customer engagement, customers are increasingly seen as a primary source of innovation, idea development, and concept testing. An increasing variety of mechanisms are being used to bring in diverse external perspectives to innovation and product development.

For more on using crowds for innovation see Chapter 22.

2 Marketing and customer engagement

Marketing is one of the most prominent applications of crowds, particularly in large organizations. The immediate use of crowds in the marketing function is most often seen to be around content creation and other ways of enhancing current functions. However more companies are recognizing that one of the best ways of driving customer engagement is to involve customers and the broader community in brand and marketing activities.

For more on using crowds for marketing see Chapter 6.

3 Processes

There are two major opportunities in applying crowds to processes. The first is in shifting existing processes to crowd-based structures. The second is in identifying value-creating processes that may previously not have been viable using internal resources. However there are significant challenges in implementing processes based on crowds.

Crowdsourcing aggregators, as described in Chapter 23, are often ideal for large organizations, as they usually include the associated professional services needed to design and run larger crowd tasks. More generally the use of microtasks is rapidly rising as a way to contain costs and expand capabilities across a variety of arenas.

In addition, an increasing number of big companies are now using service marketplaces to perform specific classes of activities and tasks. This is usually done in a less structured way than the use of microtask workers, by giving discretion to some staff to use external talent within defined parameters.

For more on using crowds for processes see in particular Chapters 17, 18, and 23.

4   Internal crowds

Companies with a large number of employees have the opportunity to consider their staff members as a crowd. This is valuable in finding ways of tapping employees' capabilities beyond their core roles. Most often this is for innovation and marketing, however there are many other applications.

Idea platforms that help to identify, filter, and action ideas from within and sometimes beyond an organization's employees have been used for well over a decade, however are gradually becoming more commonplace. Alongside these, prediction markets are well-suited to use within large companies as they need a significant minimum threshold of participation to achieve meaningful results.

Just as tapping external crowds can be very valuable for customer engagement, the use of internal crowds, done well, can have a very positive impact on staff engagement.

For more on aspects of using internal crowds see in particular Chapter 22.

5   Business models

While crowds are becoming an important aspect of the business models of many organizations, this applies differently in large and entrepreneurial organizations. While newer organizations can design their business model around crowds from the outset, established companies usually are looking to complement their existing core business models, or in some cases to evolve them into new models more relevant for a changing environment.

Large companies that have existing strategy processes often find it valuable to bring perspectives on crowd business models into their strategic planning.

For more on crowd business models see Chapter 25.

Specific issues in using crowds in enterprise

At a detail level, the success factors for using crowds are similar irrespective of the size of the organization. However there are some issues that are specifically relevant to large companies.

Culture and adoption

Large enterprise cultures are rarely open to the use of external crowds. As described in Chapter 9, a clear program that fits with existing culture change initiatives needs to be put in place. Issues around adoption will vary depending on the context and the type of crowdsourcing performed, shaping relevant initiatives.

Governance

For larger organizations governance issues need to be addressed, as there can be concerns on multiple issues including quality, capabilities, and intellectual property. Ross Dawson, co-author of this book, has addressed in his book Implementing Enterprise 2.0 and other publications the concept of "governance for transformation," in which governance must be designed and implemented so as to enable organizational transformation, as well as contain risks.

Crowdsourcing for entrepreneurial and growth business

The use of crowds by small and growing businesses is quite distinct from that by large organizations. While larger organizations in general use crowds to extend their existing capabilities, smaller organizations often use crowds for what would previously have been considered to be core functions. The issue of what functions should be done internally and externally is even more pointed than for large firms.

Creative individuals and groups in domains such as film, music, and design usually have significant financial constraints, though also often have access to broad communities, sometimes of keen fans. This supports both crowdsourcing the creative process, as well as the use of crowdfunding, which to date has been largely of creative ventures.

Service marketplaces and competition platforms are the two types of crowdsourcing most used by small and mid-sized business. There are minimal barriers to using these services, with immediate benefits in terms of broadening access to providers and achieving competitive costs.

Moving forward, it is likely that small and mid-sized businesses will start to use other types of crowdsourcing to a greater degree, supported by the emergence of platforms designed for that market. Microtasks and distributed innovation are both areas likely to experience strong growth in the smaller business market.

The very nature of smaller organizations creates many opportunities for the use of crowds. Below are some of the more prominent ones.

1 ### Software and web development
For companies where software is at the heart of their offering, crowds are becoming increasingly central to the way work is performed. Software architecture and project management are almost always maintained as core functions, however the development can be outsourced to individuals or teams. In other cases it is possible to use more sophisticated competition structures for individual software modules, or in some cases higher-level functions.

Non-technology companies that require web development often use crowd-based development. However they may find it valuable to use local developers to help interpret their needs and in some cases manage the external work required.

2 ### Design and identity
Smaller organizations less commonly have dedicated designers on staff, so the use of external designers has become extremely common. Competition platforms are now commonly used for key design tasks such as logos, business cards, and brochures.

As with other functions, it is important to balance internal and external functions, with in the case of design significant value in establishing core design parameters that can be applied to external work.

3 ### Online promotion
As smaller and growth companies increasingly rely on online promotion, there are many ways in which crowds can play an important role. Content creation and social media is often partly or wholly delegated to external talent. Search Engine Optimization (SEO) and Search Engine Marketing (SEM) activities, which in the past have tended to have been done by agencies, are now often segmented into specific tasks that can be allocated to relevant workers. As discussed in Chapter 24, SEM has proven to be a task that can be effectively given to distributed experts.

4 ### Virtual assistants
The rise of virtual assistants has been a boon to many small businesses. Virtual assistants are sometimes freelancers who divide their time among local clients, or more often workers who service global clients. Depending

on their skill levels, they can free up company executives for more valuable tasks, or sometimes help to co-ordinate broader activities or other external workers.

The issues discussed in Chapter 8 on the importance of building strong, ongoing relationships are particularly important in the use of virtual assistants.

5   Processes

The limited resources of small and growth companies means that many processes need to be under consideration to be done externally. However the limited resources can by the same token sometimes make it harder to set up those processes externally. The quality control activities and structures that large organizations are able to establish can be prohibitive for smaller companies to set up. However when those processes, such as lead generation or database maintenance, are core to the organization's success then it is often worth making the investment to enable the efficient running of those processes by crowds.

6   Business models

While large organizations usually have established business models that can be challenging to evolve, smaller and growth companies have far greater flexibility and opportunity to build crowd business models from the outset. Chapter 25 provides a framework for designing and implementing business models based on crowds, which is particularly relevant for entrepreneurial organizations.

Specific issues in using crowds in growth companies

There are some specific factors at play that need to be considered by smaller and entrepreneurial companies in how they use crowds.

Core capabilities

It is far easier for a small or growth company than an enterprise to have a significant or even dominant proportion of its activities performed outside the organization. Many companies are now stretching the boundaries of what can be done externally. As such it is particularly important to be careful of outsourcing too much.

Project supervision must be a core capability for almost all companies. This can include project management as it is traditionally understood, though it can be limited to working effectively with external project managers. In a related way, the ability to use crowds well is increasingly becoming a key success factor for growth businesses.

There are a variety of other specific decisions that need to be made on whether specific functions, such as design, product innovation, or marketing are core to the organization. The rise of crowds means that there is a far broader scope to the strategic decisions required by smaller organizations.

Culture and attitudes

In smaller organizations business owners or leaders can readily drive change and adopt new ways of working, which makes the adoption of crowdsourcing easier. There is usually a willingness for a wide range of tasks to be done externally. It is usually quite clear that effective use of external talent will create faster growth and more opportunities for employees.

Crowdsourcing for marketing

6

" A crowd is a tribe without a leader. A crowd is a tribe without communication. Most organizations spend their time marketing to the crowd. Smart organizations assemble the tribe. "

Seth Godin, author and entrepreneur

Marketing is one of the most important applications of crowdsourcing for organizations large and small. There are many ways in which external talent can be applied within existing marketing structures and processes. Perhaps more importantly, getting customers to participate in key activities including product development and communication can be one of the most powerful ways to build a stronger community engagement and brand.

Chapter overview

- Marketing is one of the fastest rising uses of crowdsourcing in business.

- There are a wide variety of applications of crowdsourced marketing, including content creation, idea generation, customer insights, and customer engagement.

- Corporate marketers and agencies can choose for specific applications to use existing platforms or build their own crowd.

- Custom crowds can be built from groups of professionals, amateurs, or customers.

- Platforms for crowdsourced marketing often focus on video production, other content creation, or customer insights and engagement.

The rise of crowdsourcing in marketing

Marketing is one of the most important business applications of crowdsourcing. Marketing is about reaching outside companies to the customers and communities that matter the most to the organization. Tapping external talent and insight is completely aligned with that mission.

Here are five of the most important reasons that crowdsourcing is becoming increasingly central to the world of marketing.

1 **More and better ideas**

Even the largest creative agencies filled with the very brightest people have limited resources compared with an open call. From a corporate client perspective, agencies often present them with excellent ideas, though only a few. Crowdsourcing can bring far more, and more diverse, ideas, though of course this does create a filtering burden. Through this approach broader reach better ideas can be brought to bear, as long the right contributors are attracted into the process.

2 **More efficient**

Every domain of business and government is being called on to do more with less. This drive to efficiency inevitably calls for new approaches. Effective crowdsourcing is not always as inexpensive as newcomers imagine, however done well and with appropriate guidance, it can provide greater efficiencies than established ways of working.

3 **Need for speed**

Companies are running on increasingly compressed time cycles in product innovation and marketing. Crowds, managed well, can generate results in marketing campaigns often more quickly than traditional approaches from corporate teams and agencies. It is however important to be careful as crowd approaches, particularly with a quality control and filtering overlay, can be less consistent in a given timeframe for some kinds of campaigns.

4 **Driving real engagement**

Crowdsourcing by its nature brings participation from many people. One of the most powerful ways of engaging customers and broader communities is by getting their contributions and participation. It is one of the strongest ways to generate positive brand engagement.

5   Increased competition

In a world flooded with media and awash with choice, companies are finding it increasingly difficult to cut through to reach customers and build meaningful engagement. Those companies that are using crowds well are gaining competitive advantage, pushing other organizations to adopt new ways of working to achieve their marketing objectives.

From the perspective of creative agencies, they are now often experiencing competition from crowdsourcing platforms or approaches. This puts them in a situation in which they may feel the need to adopt crowd-based methodologies to compete on quality and efficiency. There is also an opportunity to work with their clients in tapping crowds effectively, which in turn requires them to build experience in crowdsourcing for marketing projects.

Marketing applications of crowdsourcing

There are a wide range of applications of crowdsourcing to marketing. Seven of the most important domains are listed here.

Applications of crowdsourcing to marketing		
APPLICATION	**DESCRIPTION**	**EXAMPLES**
Content creation	Generating marketing content such as videos, images, or copy.	Doritos has run a 'Crash the Super Bowl' competition to create its Super Bowl ad every year since 2007.
Idea generation	Creating ideas to identify or develop marketing initiatives.	Sunsilk uses platform eYeka to gather ideas on marketing the next generation of its products.
Product development	Identifying insights to enhance existing products or develop new ones.	Dell Ideastorm and My Starbucks Idea offer a platform for customers to provide input into product development.
Customer insights	Gathering customer perspectives on current or potential products or marketing initiatives.	Volvo Facebook "You Inside" campaign gathers insights on what people carry in their cars.

Continued on the next page >

Applications of crowdsourcing to marketing (continued)

APPLICATION	DESCRIPTION	EXAMPLES
Customer engagement	Building greater participation and affiliation with the brand and company.	Sam Adams crowdsourced the flavor of a new beer launched at SxSW tech and music festival.
Customer advocacy	Tapping customers to spread word to their personal networks about products or services.	Procter & Gamble's Tremor's extensive community of mothers shares brand information with their personal networks.
Pricing	Gaining insights on attitudes to possible pricing strategies.	Product innovation platform Quirky uses a Pricing Game to shape its pricing strategies.

Using platforms or build own crowds

Both corporate marketers and agencies need to consider whether they should use existing platforms for crowdsourcing, or build their own crowds. The following table provides a brief summary of the key issues.

Comparison of using platforms or building own crowds

ISSUE	USE PLATFORMS	OWN CROWD
Breadth	Broad, deep pool of contributors.	Usually limited size.
Relevance	May not have right contributors.	Highly relevant contributors.
Time	Available immediately.	Significant time to develop.
Process	Can offer sophisticated filtering.	Platforms may be less flexible.
Investment	Low establishment costs	Large investment required.
Advantage	Differentiation through skilled use.	Can offer competitive advantage.

Most importantly, there is a significant time and cost required to establish a crowd. Notably, even organizations that build their own crowds over time tend to use established platforms as part of the process of attracting a relevant pool of talent. Below are some of the factors in building your own crowds or using external platforms.

Building your own crowd

If corporate marketers and agencies choose to develop their own crowds, they need first to consider who they want in the community, and how they will attract them.

Types of custom crowds for marketing

CROWD TYPE	KEY CHARACTERISTICS	EXAMPLE
Professional	• Closed community • Experienced • Significant rewards	Crowdsourced ad agency Victors & Spoils has built its own crowd of professionals (see Chapter 25).
Amateur	• Invite-only or open • Aimed at diversity • Often rewarded	PR firm Ketchum has built Mindfire, a platform for students from selected global universities to provide outside perspectives on creative solutions.
Customer	• Know the brand • Usually enthusiasts • Preferably diverse	Airline KLM has developed a closed community of loyal customers to explore new ideas for service delivery and innovation.

Using platforms

Over the last years many crowdsourcing platforms for marketing have developed, providing every organization with the ability to tap crowds. The attraction of the better-developed platforms is that they provide immediate access to crowds that are interested and engaged, and have sometimes sophisticated processes for filtering and working with contributors.

Success factors

There are a number of distinct types of platforms that are used to tap crowds for marketing initiatives. The success factors for each differ, however should be taken into consideration when starting to use these platforms.

Many crowdsourced marketing platforms use some variation on competitions to get results. In using these kinds of platforms refer to the guidelines provided in Chapter 21 on Competition Platforms. There are a few other points that are worth considering in applications for marketing.

1 **Carefully select platforms**

In addition to the more obvious issues of depth and talent of contributors on the platform, it is important to assess the processes used by the platforms. Some have simple competition structures, while others use a multi-stage process that involves getting input from broad pools of participants. The process used will impact the timeframe of projects, as well as the match to the project objectives and client working style.

2 **Offer sufficient rewards**

While offering sufficiently attractive financial and non-financial rewards is an important part of any successful competition, this is particularly important for marketing initiatives. While the overt cost of creating marketing content, for example, can be quite low, there can be a significant advantage to paying well in terms of quality, as well as brand implications. While not every company can afford the $1 million that Doritos has paid to Super Bowl winning contributors, it is almost always preferable to overpay than underpay.

3 **Consider closed contributor pools**

Some content creation platforms offer the choice of closed or open contributor pools, while others are based on one of the two models. In many cases being open to contributions from anybody can broaden the input and increase the chances of success. There are however situations in which closed pools can be preferable, including when you want professional contributors who are unlikely to participate in open calls.

4 **Be aware of potential negative response**

As discussed in Chapter 8 on Relationship Value, there are many designers who believe that running design competitions is unethical, and refuse to participate. This is not a significant issue for consumer brands who are not directly involved with designers. However for some brands it can be a real consideration. When notebook company Moleskine ran a crowdsourced logo design competition, many of the designers who are among its most devoted fans felt betrayed and turned against the brand.

Crowdsourced marketing platforms

Platforms that bring together creative communities and corporate marketers have proliferated over the last years, with many new players continuing to enter the market. The following table provides an overview of some of the many participants in this space.

The customer engagement space is becoming extremely busy, as many social business platforms are shifting their focus from internal to external communities. The companies listed below are examples only.

Examples of crowdsourced marketing platforms

NAME	HQ	NOTES
VIDEO		
GeniusRocket	U.S.	Video production with a curated crowd of professionals covering all stages of the process.
Mofilm	U.K.	Video competitions for global brands and social causes.
Poptent	U.S.	Crowdsourced video production and ideas/ concepts.
Production Party	Australia	Facilitated video production process currently focused on Australian market.
Userfarm	U.K.	Competition platform for video, operating in five languages.
Tongal	U.S.	Creative platform for video projects that go through ideation, suggestion, and production phases.
Wooshii	U.K.	Marketplace for video, animation, and rich media creatives.
Zooppa	U.S./ Italy	Facilitated crowdsourced video and design briefs process for large corporates.
OTHER CREATIVE CONTENT		
BlurGroup	U.K.	Creative services marketplace including marketing campaigns, design, content and brand ideas, now extending from marketing into other domains.
BootB	Italy	Various marketing-related briefs across multiple languages, mostly centered on Italian market.
Brandfighters	Netherlands	Dutch language marketing challenges and projects including brand ideas, content, and video.
Eyeka	France	Brands post contests around design, brand ideas, and campaigns to a global community of creative.

Continued on the next page >

Examples of crowdsourced marketing platforms (continued)

NAME	HQ	NOTES
Giant Hydra	Canada	Project teams are selected from a curated global community to work on creative briefs.
Jovoto	Germany	Creative community collaborates on briefs relating to design, brand and product ideas, and marketing.
Talenthouse	U.S.	Creative briefs around art, design, fashion, film, music and photography.

CUSTOMER INSIGHTS AND ENGAGEMENT

NAME	HQ	NOTES
BzzAgent	U.S.	Recruits crowds for insights on brand campaigns and enlists them as brand advocates.
Chaordix	Canada	Platform for crowdsourcing market intelligence and innovation and building brand loyalty.
ClickAdvisor	U.K.	Engage crowds to provide market research for brands by "extracting customer wisdom".
Communispace	U.S.	Helps set up online community spaces for brands to gain consumer insights and market research.
CrowdTap	U.S.	Provides a "social marketing platform" to connect brands to groups of passionate consumers for insights and peer influence.
Passenger	U.S.	Platform for online communities for corporates to gain customer insights and "brand intelligence".

Crowdsourcing for media and content

7

> *The time for debate is over. Newspapers need to be digital first in everything they do, and more than that, they need to take the same approach to their businesses that many web-based startups have, and that means being transparent, crowdsourced, collaborative and flat.*
>
> **John Paton**, CEO, The Journal Register

Over the last years crowds have moved to the fore in many aspects of media and content creation. That shift is very likely to continue, making capabilities in tapping crowds a core competence for media companies. As different elements of the media process are broken out for crowd participation, there will be many highly valued roles for journalists and other media professionals to complement broader amateur participation. The rise of crowds in media has the potential to create a richer media landscape for all.

Chapter overview

- Crowds and crowdsourcing are at the heart of the recent and current massive shifts in the media landscape.

- We identify 12 distinct domains to which crowds can be applied in the media and news process.

- There are also a range of ways in which crowdsourcing can be applied to content businesses.

- It is critical to understand the varying motivations for crowd members to participate in media and content creation.

- There can be significant costs to effectively attracting and managing crowd contributions.

Crowds and media

The rise of crowds provides us with the single most useful perspective to understand the radically changing landscape of media over the last two decades. The shift to crowds shaping media has been seen across many dimensions, most obviously the rise of social media, which has turned hundreds of millions of people from media consumers to media creators. This has vastly broadened the scope of media from just traditional broadcasters and publishers, to an extraordinary spectrum of sizes, styles, and formats of media outlets today.

The most evident role of the crowd is in social media and micro-niche publications. However it is critical to see the breadth of ways in which crowds have moved to the center of 'mainstream' media structures and processes.

Categories of crowdsourcing media and content

Through this book we seek to cover the diversity and breadth of crowdsourcing. Too many people see one aspect of crowdsourcing and think it is the whole. In a similar way, there are many ways in which crowdsourcing can be applied to media and content businesses, and it is important to understand that diversity and the different characteristics of each space.

Domains for crowdsourcing media

Crowds are undoubtedly transforming news and journalism. However this does not mean that traditional skills, capabilities, and processes are no longer relevant. The future of media lies largely in combining established media skills with the vast capabilities of crowd participants, many of whom are highly skilled.

This is sometimes described as "pro-am" journalism, bringing together professionals and amateurs to achieve things that they could not separately. As such, in order to design and implement effective crowdsourced news and media, it is important to segment the aspects that can be performed well by crowds, usually as a complement to established processes and structures.

We identify 12 domains in which crowdsourcing can be effectively applied to news and media.

Domains for crowdsourcing media

APPLICATION	DESCRIPTION	EXAMPLES
Reporting	On-the-spot reporting and information, often as news happens.	• Twitter as frequent medium for on-the-spot breaking news reporting. • CNN's long-standing iReport gathering contributions on breaking and broader topics.
Investigation	Gathering information relating to specific questions and issues.	• Crowds helping open source platform Help Me Investigate on specific investigations. • Sunlight Foundation use of crowds to identify lobbyists in Senate hearings.
Data gathering	Collecting information on the ground.	• WNYC's requests for cost of consumer staples across New York City. • Ipaidabribe initiative in India to chronicle bribe paying.
Data sifting	Going through large data releases to identify newsworthy issues.	• The Guardian's analysis of MP expenses and documentation with Hillsborough report.
Story selection	Selecting the most interesting, relevant, and appropriate content.	• Slashdot's use of established community members to select headline stories. • Cheezburger Network's crowd selection from 500,000 submissions each month.
Fact checking	Checking facts in articles before or after publication	• Social news site Reddit's fact-checking of the 2012 Presidential debates • TruthSquad initiative to crowdsource fact checking.

Continued on the next page >

Domains for crowdsourcing media (continued)		
APPLICATION	DESCRIPTION	EXAMPLES
Story compilation	Weaving a story through selection of quotes and content.	▪ Storify platform to select social media posts, for example on Aurora shooting. ▪ Vyclone app to mix multiple video perspectives on an event.
Writing	Contribution of completed articles.	▪ Desert Connect attracts and publishes "values-driven" writers. ▪ Huffington Post has over 2,000 paid writers with many more unpaid writers.
Video	Contribution of live or recorded video, usually of news events.	▪ Cell Journalist often receives over 10,000 video contributions of extreme weather events.
Copyediting	Correcting and improving written grammar and language.	▪ Soylent add-in to Microsoft Word that allows Mechanical Turk workers to improve copy as it is being written.
Metadata	Identifying relevant tags or descriptive data to content	▪ Members of BBC online community check and add metadata to World Service radio archive. ▪ SpeakerText crowdsourced transcription of videos.
Funding	Crowdfunding journalistic initiatives.	▪ Science investigative magazine Matter raises $140,000 on Kickstarter

Domains for crowdsourcing content

Crowdsourced content such as data and opinions is fairly distinct from the media in a traditional sense. There are different dynamics at play in terms of the kind of content contributed, motivations for contributions, and the business models.

Our Crowd Business Models framework described in Chapter 25 includes a category on media and data, which provides a useful overview of how business models are structured in particularly non-media content.

Types of crowdsourced content

APPLICATION	EXAMPLES
Reference content	Wikipedia Medpedia
Databases	IMDB Data.com
Reviews and ratings	TripAdvisor Amazon.com
Questions and answers	Quora Yahoo Answers
Health experiences	PatientsLikeMe CureTogether

Generating and managing crowd contributions

There is a massive amount of external contribution to media and content organizations, in a very wide range of formats and guises. This certainly does not mean that it is easy to attract contributions. The bulk of crowd energy and input goes to a relatively small number of media outlets. Established media brands generally find it far easier to attract contributors, through the size of their audience and their reputation. However many smaller players have been very successful in attracting participation by crowds.

Motivations for contributing

There are a wide variety of motivations for contributing to media or content initiatives. There is almost always a combination of motivations for contributing. These will vary widely depending on the specific initiative and the individual.

Motivations for contributing media and content

MOTIVATION	ISSUES / EXPLANATION
Financial	Many contributors of quality content are primarily motivated by financial rewards. However acceptable pay levels are often significantly below professional rates.
Being paid	For aspiring content creators, there can be strong motivation in being a "paid writer", even if the amount of money involved is not significant.
In-kind rewards	Rewards such as access to media content or a database in return for being a contributor are well accepted.
Personal brand	Having the contributor's name and possibly bio publicly associated with their contribution can enhance their profile or reputation.
Links	Often contributors of content will be sufficiently rewarded by a link (preferably a chosen text link) from a well-ranked website as it supports their visibility in search engines.
Social impact	Some contributors are seeking opportunities to have a positive social impact, for example through sharing values or assisting social initiatives.
Contribution to commons or community	Many are motivated to contribute to what they consider a common good, such as reviews that assist better buying decisions, or compiling an open-access database. There is also often a desire to contribute to specific communities, both geographical and interest-based.
Skill development	Writers or video creators may be motivated by being able to improve their capabilities, and will value coaching or editorial feedback.

Managing contributions

Media companies that see the dream of crowdsourced content are often oblivious to the amount of work required to effectively manage crowdsourced contributions. Through this book, notably in Chapters 17 and 18, we focus on the realities and costs of quality assurance.

For example, the BBC's UGC Hub which deals with user-generated content has around 20 staff. They have a wide range of responsibilities, but essentially it is to gather and filter crowd-contributed content. While there is certainly enormous value in those external contributions, the cost of making them usable is significant.

PART III

BUILDING RELATIONSHIPS

8 Relationship value

9 Changing organizations

CROWD BUSINESS MODELS — VIII

USING OTHER PLATFORMS — VII

CROWDFUNDING — VI

MANAGING PROJECTS — V

USING SERVICE MARKETPLACES — IV

BUILDING RELATIONSHIPS — III

APPLICATIONS OF CROWDSOURCING — II

FUNDAMENTALS OF CROWDS — I

Relationship value

8

Working with crowds who are usually working remotely can have a dehumanizing effect. It is important to value the people you work with in the crowd, and recognize that giving respect and building valued relationships with them will lead to the best outcomes for your business. We cannot ignore the ethical dimensions of crowdsourcing, but must understand the issues and act in accord with our beliefs.

Chapter overview

- The key principles of successful crowdsourcing are respect, relationships, rewards, and roles.

- Most of the value in tapping crowds will come from attracting the best to work for you.

- The non-financial rewards that providers may value include flexibility, consistent revenue, interesting work, and learning and development.

- Ethical issues in crowdsourcing include how much workers are paid, taking jobs offshore, and unpaid submissions to competitions.

Key principles of crowdsourcing

Crowdsourcing and service marketplaces are new to many people, so they are often unsure how best to approach them. Some seem to think it is all about getting things done at the lowest cost possible. However anyone taking that approach is unlikely to get good results. Much of the value of tapping an entire world of providers is getting the most talented to contribute to business endeavors.

Following are a set of key principles that we believe provide the best foundation for creating value using crowds.

Respect

Perhaps the most fundamental principle of successful crowdsourcing is respect. Being able to draw on the most talented people is the most valuable aspect of a connected world. Simply to recognize that talent requires an underlying attitude of respect, and clearly the most talented will only be interested in working in relationships of respect. Respect will lead to greater value creation in all business relationships.

Relationships

Transaction costs have gone down immensely. Yet there are still significant costs to finding the best people and building the mutual knowledge out of which efficient, effective work stems. Building relationships reduces these transaction costs to zero. Those who are able to build strong relationships with their providers will be able to attract the best, and efficiently create highly scalable organizations.

Rewards

The initial attraction to crowdsourcing for many businesspeople is the potential to reduce costs. While this is a valid objective, minimizing fees paid rarely leads to optimal outcomes. The primary issue should be identifying the rewards that will attract the best talent for the job. For many, those rewards are primarily financial. However there are many non-financial rewards that are also important, including flexibility, consistency, learning, good relationships, and interesting work.

Roles

Crowdsourcing is a central aspect of the powerful shift to distributed work. This is changing how organizations work, and their roles and structures. To effectively tap the new resources available through crowd-based work, organizations need to clearly identify and specify roles within their companies and in the crowd. Tapping the value of crowds requires clarifying these roles and building new working structures that span organizational boundaries.

Getting the best

There is a vast range of work that can be performed by crowds, extending organizations' capabilities beyond those of their staff. As discussed in Chapter 4 on When to use crowds, some of that work is commoditized while other work needs the best available talent.

In a global connected economy in which work flows increasingly freely, a good working definition of talent is those who have the luxury of choosing who they work for. These are people who want interesting challenges and to work with people who are pleasant to deal with.

Those who view crowdsourcing primarily as a way to pay less for work will never attract the best providers. A different attitude and approach is required to get not just the best providers, but even those who are simply good.

Attracting good providers is just the first step. There remains the challenge of getting the best out of them. Different clients will get different quality results from the same provider, driven by a variety of factors including how well they communicate, and the degree to which they can inspire the provider to genuinely care about the project outcomes.

Understanding provider objectives

The heart of attracting the best providers and getting the best from them is understanding what they want, and doing your best to create value for them. Any relationship is a two-way street. If you can consistently create value for others, you will find you are able to attract the best people and build constructive long-term relationships with them.

Below are some of the most important and common objectives for crowd participants. The issue of non-financial value and how to reward people beyond payment is covered in more detail in Chapter 14 on Rewarding. If you can help your providers to achieve their objectives, you will undoubtedly get better work and will engender loyalty that makes them place your work as a top priority.

Consistent revenue

Almost every freelancer has both to get work and do work. Getting a single job is good, however once it ends they then need to bring in more work. Obtaining reasonably consistent work gives far more comfort in managing their finances and not being under continual pressure to get new work.

Manageable schedule

Providers have to deal not only with clients who consistently want all work done yesterday, but also fluctuations in the amount of work coming in, meaning they can sometimes be overwhelmed. Considering your priorities and deadlines and clearly communicating these is extremely valuable to providers. Respect providers' time, and do not put them under time pressure unless absolutely necessary.

Interesting and challenging work

The smarter and more talented the individual, the more they will be motivated by doing interesting tasks. Mundane work simply pays the bills, whereas challenging projects are stimulating, exciting, and help them to develop new skills and perspectives. The feeling of contributing to an interesting project is a significant reward for talented workers.

Learning and development

In a rapidly changing world, everybody needs to continually develop their skills, or see their market value erode. Freelancers can learn and develop their capabilities through challenging work, doing new kinds of work, training, and working with challenging clients who help them take their capabilities to new levels.

Good working relationships

Just as the attitudes and working style of your direct manager and colleagues will shape the quality of your working life, freelancers' lives are shaped by how their clients work and communicate with them. Understand the impact you have on others' lives, and recognize that anyone reasonably talented will avoid working with unpleasant people.

 I think we have a duty, as people who live in a relatively wealthy country, to free up all of this talent waiting in the wings and ready to participate in the global economy. We have to connect that talent to genuine opportunity.
Leila Janah, Founder, Samasource

Ethics of crowdsourcing

Many people's first reaction to hearing about crowdsourcing is to raise the ethical issues. Certainly a non-ethical approach to crowdsourcing can result in a negative impact on people's lives and potentially beyond. However it is also important to understand that a shift to crowd-based work is an inevitable implication of a connected world.

There are no clear answers. Everyone needs to be aware of the issues, and act in line with their own beliefs as to what is appropriate, and how they wish to work with crowds.

Following are a series of points giving different perspectives on some of the most important ethical issues raised by crowdsourcing.

Ethical issues in crowdsourcing

	POINT	COUNTERPOINT
People should be paid for their contributions to for-profit ventures	If crowd contributions help to create profits, contributors should share in those profits. For example, Huffington Post's sale to AOL should benefit the many unpaid workers who helped to create that value. In other cases, insidious companies present work as for the common good when they are actually going to profit from it.	Unpaid contributions are always voluntary. They are done because there are other forms of value, such as exposure, learning, or simply spending time in an interesting fashion. It is the choice of contributors, who can make informed decisions on what they wish to contribute to.
It is exploitation to pay people very low amounts	Simply finding the lowest-cost worker in the world amounts to exploitation. These people do not have any negotiating power, and developed world rich are paying them ridiculously low pay.	Connected work adds to the very limited range of opportunities available to people in the developing world. Despite the low pay by developed world standards, it is usually more lucrative than local alternatives, and individuals can often choose their working conditions and hours more than they would be able to in a local factory.
Businesses should support their countries and communities by employing locally	Businesses have an obligation to their employees and community to employ locally. It is unethical simply to go to the lowest-cost provider in the world, without regard for those around you. Just as most companies hope and expect their local community to support them, they also should support their local community, even if it means paying more. Companies that consistently offshore jobs and work will destroy the local economy and in turn destroy themselves.	An increasing proportion of companies are experiencing global competition. If they do not use the best talent at the lowest cost, they will not be competitive and risk going out of business. If they remain successful businesses they will hire as many if not more local people, as the reality is that many roles cannot be outsourced. We should also not forget that we are part of a global community. Crowdsourcing provides an unparalleled opportunity for talented people in developing countries to make far more money than they could where they live, creating greater prosperity for themselves and helping their countries and local communities to grow.

Continued on the next page >

Ethical issues in crowdsourcing (continued)

	POINT	COUNTERPOINT
Professionals should not do unpaid work	The 'No Spec' movement, born in the designer community but now stretching beyond it, says that all creative work should be paid. Asking for work that will only be paid for if the client likes it is unethical. Design competitions, for example, where many submit their work but only one gets paid, are reprehensible. Creative professionals should commit to never participate in 'spec' work, as it is undermining the entire industry and the livelihoods of many.	There are many reasons why professionals may choose to participate in competitions. Sometimes they can make a living from winning a sufficient number of the often relatively low prizes on offer, in other cases they find it an opportunity to develop their skills and create work that, if they lose, they can still use for other clients. Certainly designers have the choice of not participating in competitions, and the reality is that the best designers do not. Clients who want the absolute best must work with them on a different basis. However there are sufficient designers who freely choose to participate in the competition platforms to make them a viable option for clients.

Changing organizations

9

> ❝ There is nothing more difficult to take in hand, more perilous to conduct, or more uncertain in its success, than to take the lead in the introduction of a new order of things. ❞
>
> **Niccolo Machiavelli**,
> Italian historian, philosopher, humanist, and writer

The opportunities created by crowdsourcing do not always come easily for established businesses. Companies need to change how they work, which may impact employees' roles and responsibilities as well as business processes. Companies need to carefully manage the journey from recognizing the benefits of crowdsourcing through to embedding these approaches into their operations.

Chapter overview

- Resistance to the introduction of crowdsourcing approaches can be expected if the primary strategic intent is to cut costs and reduce headcount.

- Strategies that are driven by generating positive momentum to the organization and its employees' careers will generate more value and help to gain support from staff.

- There are a wide variety of concerns commonly raised, including confidentiality, quality of output, loss of jobs, and the relevance of crowdsourcing to the organization.

- Steps to driving adoption include creating a sense of urgency, communicating clear policies, doing pilot projects, defining roles, and providing training.

Dealing with resistance to crowdsourcing

Any organization that adopts crowdsourcing approaches needs to be prepared for internal resistance. Some of this may be a response to change in general, however there can be specific concerns about the introduction of crowd-based work.

The validity of these concerns will depend on the organization's strategic intent of the use of crowdsourcing. If the intention is simply to cut costs through headcount reduction, the resistance is to be expected, and trying to present the initiative for something other than what it is will not help the situation. In this case there will undoubtedly be many broader organizational challenges than just introducing the use of crowdsourcing. In addition, using crowds to replace staff is unlikely to be a realistic or useful objective.

Where the intent of using crowdsourcing is positive, in terms of benefiting the growth of the organization and its staff, people's spoken and unspoken concerns may have varying degrees of validity, but can always be effectively addressed.

Many perceive the use of crowds as primarily a tool for driving efficiencies and lower costs, however even this can be reframed as an opportunity for individuals. Creating more efficient processes can free up resources to enhance current operations and generate new revenue opportunities, as well as create new possibilities for staff.

In many cases the most valuable uses of crowdsourcing have nothing to do with cost but rather create insight and outcomes that could not have been available by any other means. Genuinely approaching the use of crowds in terms of positives for the organization and employees is the only sustainable way to turn resistance into support.

Here are some of the primary areas of concerns usually expressed when crowdsourcing approaches are introduced.

Concerns and responses on the use of crowdsourcing		
	CONCERN	RESPONSE
Confidentiality	Confidential information or intellectual property will be exposed externally and stolen.	These are genuine issues, which is why clear policies and work processes have been established to minimize risks.
Quality of output	Services provided will be unreliable, untrustworthy, or not meet deadlines.	Structured processes for selecting providers and managing quality control will ensure appropriate quality, and identify ways to continually improve this.

Continued on the next page >

Concerns and responses on the use of crowdsourcing (continued)

	CONCERN	RESPONSE
Costs of using crowds	There will be significant costs to changing work processes and using them effectively.	It is true that in some cases the costs of using crowds will outweigh the savings, and sometimes even the other benefits. Crowds will only be used where there is real value created.
Change to roles	Job descriptions will change, disrupting work and requiring learning new skills.	Certainly, roles will change and new skills may be required. This is an intrinsic aspect of work in a changing world.
Loss of jobs	Current jobs in the organization could be lost.	The strategic intent of the use of crowds is not to reduce staff, but to create more value for the organization and new opportunities for employees.
Changed external relationships	Existing relationships with service providers will change.	In some cases existing providers will be replaced with new providers or crowds, creating the opportunity to build new relationships.
Immaturity	Crowdsourcing is new and not ready for use by mainstream organizations.	Crowdsourcing has been used by governments and corporations for literally centuries, and some manifestations of crowd work, such as open source software, are now well-established in the world's largest organizations. While crowdsourcing is still evolving, significant benefits come from early adoption.
Inappropriate to organization	Crowdsourcing is only used by start-ups and technology-based organizations.	Large corporations such as Procter & Gamble, Starbucks, Pfizer, and Dell as well as many government organizations are using crowdsourcing approaches extensively.
Lack of need	Current work processes are well-established and do not need to be changed.	The pace of change in the business landscape means we must innovate now in how we work rather than being forced to catch up later.
Best resources are available internally	We have all the skills and talent we need inside the organization.	Today no organization has all the skills it requires, and is at a competitive disadvantage if it only uses internal resources.

Supporting adoption

If you are bringing crowdsourcing into an organization you need to consider the potential resistance and whether there are particular measures you can take to facilitate adoption. This will depend on the culture of the organization and the initial approaches you are taking to the use of crowdsourcing. In some or even many cases, there will be no significant resistance or issues with adoption. In other cases strategies for adoption will need to be considered and implemented.

> " *If you want to teach people a new way of thinking, don't bother trying to teach them. Instead, give them a tool, the use of which will lead to new ways of thinking.* "
>
> **Buckminster Fuller**, inventor and author

6 steps to adoption of crowdsourcing

There are 6 steps that businesses can take to overcome resistance and improve adoption of crowdsourcing approaches:

1 **Create a sense of urgency**

There needs to be a sense of urgency for organizations to embrace game-changing shifts. Use existing communication channels, particularly from senior management and in larger staff meetings, to highlight the actions taken and the reasons. These should always be framed in terms of benefits to the organization and staff. Ideally you are looking to create not just a feeling of the need to use crowdsourcing, but a positive outlook on the benefits and possibilities. It is valid to frame organizational survival as well as success as a benefit.

2 **Communicate a clear strategy**

The organization's leadership needs to define the role of crowdsourcing in the organization, including the benefits and scope. As described in Chapter 4, a key issue is gaining clarity on and communicating what will remain inside in the organization, and what may be done externally. A clear policy on crowdsourcing could include:

- The strategic rationale for crowdsourcing and the resulting benefits
- Specific tasks where crowdsourcing will be implemented or trialed
- Approved providers or platforms (where relevant)
- Crowdsourcing approval processes
- Information sharing policies

Further details on implementing relevant organizational processes and structures are described in Chapter 18.

3 **Start small, learn, iterate**

Establishing pilot projects is one of the best ways to identify the best approaches and their applicability to particular tasks or parts of the organization. Success factors for pilots include careful selection of the pilot project staff, designing for specific benefits, actively identifying lessons learned, and building project visibility. It is also important to cut off or significantly modify pilots that are not working well, as well as rapidly building on any successes.

4 **Define roles and provide training**

Establishing clear roles and structures, as described in detail in Chapter 18, enables people to understand their role and how that relates to other internal and external staff. This includes any workflow, approval processes, or other new aspects of their work. Especially for anyone who will have significant responsibility for the use of crowdsourcing platforms or external providers, training or mentoring should be provided. This book can be used as an introduction and guide.

5 **Design incentives**

Organizations should define metrics to measure the benefits of crowdsourcing. These may be as simple as time saved or may include benefits generated through the use of crowds. Incentives for staff on the effective use of crowdsourcing can be included in compensation or bonuses, or be addressed in staff reviews. Alternatively, discretionary bonuses or incentives can be used to support a positive stance to the use of crowd-based approaches.

6 **Highlight successes**

Stories of successful employment of crowdsourcing should be communicated across the organization to increase interest, and reward those who are early adopters. These stories make the benefits tangible, motivate staff, and allow useful insights to be shared across the organization.

PART IV

USING SERVICE MARKETPLACES

CROWD BUSINESS MODELS VIII

USING OTHER PLATFORMS VII

CROWDFUNDING VI

MANAGING PROJECTS V

USING SERVICE MARKETPLACES IV

BUILDING RELATIONSHIPS III

APPLICATIONS OF CROWDSOURCING II

FUNDAMENTALS OF CROWDS I

Fundamentals of service marketplaces

10

> *" We believe more and more companies will adopt the hybrid model of distributed work. Some businesses will have about 30% of staff working onsite and 70% working online. Workers are embracing online work because it offers them independence, one-minute commutes and more control over their careers.*
>
> **Fabio Rosati**, CEO, Elance

Service marketplaces are playing a vital role in facilitating the rapid shift to global distributed work. As billions of workers around the world become internet-enabled, a significant proportion of them highly talented, this provides a vast pool of labor that companies around the world can tap. However getting great results from service marketplaces is not always as easy as it can initially seem. Following structured process and developing specific capabilities provide a sound foundation for getting great results.

Chapter overview

- Service marketplaces bring together a potential pool of billions of workers and hundreds of millions of companies.

- They are not just marketplaces, but also provide an array of tools and processes to facilitate effective virtual work.

- Other terms used to describe this phenomenon include cloud work, labor-on-demand, freelance markets, and individual outsourcing.

- We introduce the elements of the service marketplace process and key capabilities required that will be covered through Part III of this book.

Understanding service marketplaces

Around the world there are literally billions of workers, a significant and increasing proportion of them with access to the Internet, and over one hundred million companies that employ workers. There is clearly immense value in bringing together these companies and workers in a structured way. This is what service marketplaces do.

The five largest global service marketplaces are Elance, Freelancer.com, Guru.com, oDesk, and vWorker.com, with many others including some just below this top tier. Collectively these companies have paid over $1 billion to workers around the world. An overview of the key features of each of the major platforms can be found in Chapter 16.

As discussed in Chapter 1, some argue that service marketplaces are not true crowdsourcing, as work is done by individuals or small teams rather than distilling the wisdom of many. However the use of service marketplaces is today the primary way in which the power of crowd work is having an impact.

All of the major service marketplaces emphasize their work management processes and structures, including communication, collaboration, project management, structured payments, and reporting. As such their role is not just one of matching buyers and sellers of services, but more broadly that of facilitating global distributed work.

 The space still has a long way to go. This will have a profound impact on the way we live and work.

Lukas Biewald, CEO, CrowdFlower

Other names for service marketplaces

While we believe that the best term to describe this phenomenon is 'service marketplace', there is no commonly-accepted description. Other terms used include:

- Labor-on-demand
- Cloud work
- Distributed labor
- Virtual workplace
- Human cloud
- Individual outsourcing
- Work marketplace
- Freelance market

Conceptual diagram of service marketplaces

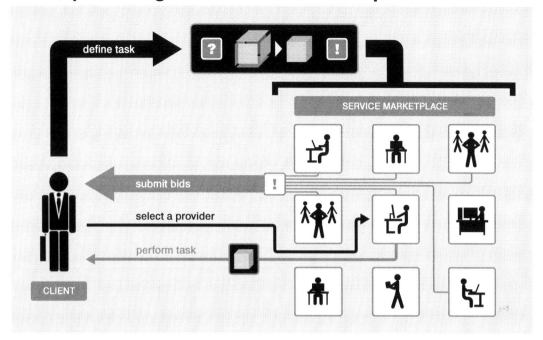

The service marketplace process

In Part IV of this book we explore in detail the process of successfully using service marketplaces. Below are the primary tasks in using a service marketplace, together with the chapter in which they are covered. While the significant number of activities involved in the service marketplace process may make it seem complex, in many cases these can be done very swiftly, particularly once the user has built experience. Some activities, such as running trials, are optional steps to enhance outcomes in specific situations.

ACTIVITY	CHAPTER
Define tasks and outcomes	11
Select the marketplace	11
Write the job specification	11
Set fees levels and rewards	11,14
Select hourly or fixed fees	11
Select candidates	12
Interview candidates	12

Continued on the next page >

ACTIVITY (continued)	CHAPTER
Run trials	12
Hire the provider	12
Set milestones	13
Establish agreements	13
Monitor performance	13
Make payment	15
Give and receive feedback	15

Developing capabilities

In addition to following the service marketplace process and learning how to do that better, there are a number of more general capabilities that are relevant particularly for getting results on service marketplaces, and often more generally across other crowdsourcing platforms. Here are some of the key capabilities that should be developed to achieve great outcomes, and the chapters where these topics are covered, sometimes in other Parts of the book.

CAPABILITY	CHAPTER
Find talented providers	12
Build relationships	8,14
Communicate clearly	13
Set safeguards	13
Create non-financial rewards	14
Develop providers	14
Disengaging	15
Manage projects	17
Establish structures and processes	19
Manage organizational change	9

Specifying

11

> *Be anal about the details. It pays to put in time and effort upfront in project definition and wherever possible, solid examples of what you're seeking.*
>
> **Rand Fishkin**, CEO, SEOmoz

A fundamental skill in using service marketplaces is the ability to scope and describe your projects accurately so you can attract the best people. There is some effort involved in creating real clarity on what you want from your projects, but it is well worthwhile as it will drive your success, and avoid wasted time, money, and effort.

Chapter overview

- Scope projects by focusing on overall objectives and then defining outcomes, timetables, measures, and major milestones.

- Explore the service marketplaces and find one that suits your requirements.

- Develop and write a clear job specification to place on the marketplace.

- Define a target cost for the job and consider whether it should be charged as fixed fee or on a per hour basis.

CASE STUDY

Mike O'Hagan's methodology for writing job descriptions for simple tasks

Mike O'Hagan is the founder of successful moving company MiniMovers. He's used marketplaces for global talent extensively to grow his business.

"Some people are absolutely hopeless at transferring a task through the internet to another person. They write it up and it's written in such a way that is difficult to understand. The number of times you get stuff back and you think hang on, yes that is what was asked for but it's not really what I thought I was going to get!

I have a set process for describing a single task. When I need to get something done, such as a piece of graphic design or finding a list of businesses to find, I write it out in simple English so that a nine year old could understand exactly what I want.

For example it might be 'what I want is somebody to go into this and that website, I then want you to go and find these set of things here and then take this bit of information and put them in an Excel spreadsheet under these columns."

So I write out the whole job in a flowing pattern. I don't use boxes and I don't use diagrams, I write it out as a story.

When I finish that story and it makes sense and it's easy to understand I then edit it down to a shortened version which takes all the identifiers out of it.

So now I'll say I need someone to go into various websites and take certain information and put it into some columns which I will nominate in a spreadsheet. So I generalize it and I shorten it.

I then take that short generalized description and that's what I put up on oDesk as the job."

Mike O'Hagan, Owner, MiniMovers

Defining tasks and outcomes

Defining outcomes and tasks from the outset is critical for the success of any crowd-based project. The clearer you are from the beginning, the easier it is to identify the role required, write an accurate job description, hire a great provider, and ultimately develop a crowd capability that can help grow your business.

Identify overall objectives

When initiating a project the starting point should be to identify your overall objectives. Some of these will be the higher-order business outcomes, for example increasing revenue by increasing website traffic and improving brand awareness.

You should also think about your objectives around potential long-term relationships with providers. Your needs may be purely short term, for example getting a logo designed, but you may also soon need to get a new website created. This suggests an additional objective could be to identify an outstanding graphic designer you can build a relationship with and use as required for your business.

If you are relatively new to crowdsourcing it would also be worth setting an objective of learning from your experience and developing your capability in using service marketplaces.

Focus on project outcomes

It is critical to be as clear as possible on the outcomes you want from the project. From defining the overall objectives the link to the business impact should be clear. Wherever possible make these measurable or otherwise able to be assessed objectively.

Define output

You need to know what the outputs from the project will be and more specifically what they will look like. In some cases you will have a clear understanding from the outset as to what they will be. However you may need input or guidance in defining outputs in detail. For example if you are a non-technical business owner you may start by knowing you want "a new website", which after research becomes "a wordpress site with a custom theme", and thereafter a clearly specified project with a set number of pages, defined content, and established features.

Define timetable

Having a timeline upfront for the delivery of your project is critical. Even if you are relatively relaxed about it, resist the temptation to be vague on delivery dates. Deadlines keep the project focused and also allow providers to co-ordinate your project with work for other clients.

Define measures

Define measures of the success of the project that relate to your overall objectives. Some of these may be obvious, for example the percentage rise in traffic to your website. You may also want to try to calculate the time and cost saved by doing the job on service marketplaces compared to working internally or with existing suppliers.

Define major milestones

Breaking down larger projects into manageable chunks is an important issue that is covered in more detail in Chapter 13 on Setting Frameworks. However there may be obvious major milestones that you can put into your job description. For example you may identify a first step in the project of defining and agreeing on a wireframe and mockup of the website, followed by working with a third party designer, creating a website for review, and finally launching the site.

Selecting the marketplace

There are a variety of major service marketplaces available, each with distinct characteristics, and to a certain degree different providers. All of them are rapidly growing in the talent pool they give access to, and are continually introducing new features to improve the user experience.

You are more than likely to have good providers applying for roles you advertise on any of the major marketplaces. We have included a brief overview of the marketplaces in Chapter 16 to provide a starting point to assess the platforms, and below are some criteria in which they may differ. If you are expecting to be a significant user of the platforms then the best approach is to try several to see which ones have the best providers for your kind of work and the most intuitive user interfaces for you. If you will be using them less frequently, then post a job on one and you can always try another one.

Criteria for choosing different platforms	
Specialist or general	Most marketplaces are general in nature and cover all kinds of jobs such as programming, marketing, administration, and design. There are some that are particularly strong in areas such as web development, or may be dedicated to one type of work. Usually it is worth starting off on a general marketplace.
Reach	Some marketplaces have a strong geographical bias, for example featuring more US-based providers or being focused on a specific country. Some of the marketplaces provide an analysis of the location of their registered providers so you can make comparisons.

Continued on the next page >

Criteria for choosing different platforms (continued)	
Features	There are a variety of useful features on each platform which can help you operationally. These include a variety of collaboration and monitoring tools, team rooms, and easy payment of providers. All of the platforms are consistently adding more useful features so check the latest.
Charging model	The fees from the marketplaces are generally similar – between 7 and 10% on each transaction – but some provide different models for frequent users.
Hourly or fixed fee model	Marketplaces usually handle both types of jobs, but some have more developed features for hourly payments.
Recommendations	Speak to other users if you can. Personal recommendations and experiences will give you direct insights.

Writing the job specification

The job specification is critical. It's your chance to attract the best people so you want to make sure that you get the right messages across. The best providers will only apply for what seem like the most attractive opportunities.

Full specifications versus public specifications

In some cases you may be happy to share full project details with the public. More often you will prefer not to provide every aspect of the job on the service marketplace if it is publicly advertised. This is not an issue if you are only inviting existing trusted providers to bid, however by default your job post will be openly visible to all, including your competitors if they care to have a look.

The best approach is to write a full specification, which provides all necessary details to get the job done. After having created that, you create a summary specification for public posting. If you are asking for a fixed price bid, then the summary needs to provide sufficient information on the work scope for the provider to quote accurately. Since you will often not share any raw files in the public posting, you may need to describe their content in detail.

If it is difficult to give an accurate idea of the project scope without the full specification, you can ask for preliminary bids, and then select a few providers to which you provide the full specification, possibly with a Non-Disclosure Agreement, for them to finalize their bid.

Issues in writing job specifications

Clearly define project outcomes	A clear description of the outcomes of the project will make sure you're not misunderstood. In particular fixed fee jobs require sufficient information for providers to propose a fee, and for it to be unambiguous when the job is complete.
Distinguish full and public specifications	As described above, where appropriate write a full specification which is then summarized into a specification for public posting.
Use simple language	Your provider might not be using their native language to communicate with you, so use clear language and a limited vocabulary.
Ask for specific responses	Asking for very specific responses in applications (e.g. relevant experience or suggested technology platforms) helps to assess the relevance of their capabilities and understanding. It also means you can immediately discard applications from providers who haven't read and responded to the job post.
Describe the hiring processes	Let providers know if there are going to be trial tasks and interviews and the format at each step, so this is clear from the outset.
Strike a positive tone	Make sure you frame the job description in positive language, which will suggest you are good to work with and the project will be enjoyable.
Make value clear	Ensure that you mention any attractive non-financial rewards that could be valuable to bidders. These include offering flexibility, providing ongoing regular work, and public attribution of their work.
Inspire	Make your organization and the work sound inspiring and exciting. What are the possibilities, where is it going in the future, and why is this a worthwhile project?
Choose the correct categories	Marketplaces use standard keywords to describe the type of job. Make sure you select the right description to make it visible to the relevant providers.
Mention practicalities	Mention any issues important to you such as preferred time zones, software platforms, or methods of communicating.
Time frames	Make sure you mention the time frames of the project so that providers know what you expect of their availability.

> " *Your planning and organization are key to getting what you want out of it.* "
>
> **Tracey Corcoran**, Co-Founder, iPilates

Developing specifications

There are a variety of sources of guidance or inspiration you can draw on in developing useful and relevant specifications.

Research other job specifications

The best starting point is to research other job specifications across the marketplaces, especially from experienced employers who have posted many successful jobs. However do not copy these unless you fully understand their intent. Only draw out what is directly applicable to your situation.

Some of the marketplaces have a clarification board on which providers have asked questions about specifications. These give useful clues on the common gaps in specifications where providers need more details in order to bid.

Use or edit templates

Some of the service marketplaces have very good help sections that include templates and model job descriptions. These are rarely what you will want to use for your job unless it is very generic, but they provide a good starting point for you to edit and make relevant to your situation. These usually cover the major issues you are likely to want to address.

Engage a specialist

If it the job description is technical and you do not have the in-house expertise required to create a specification then you can engage a specialist to help you shape the specification. This can be done by engaging someone for an hour to discuss your situation and provide suggestions, or asking them to write the full specification. Language skills will be important in both situations. Talented providers will often be happy to help create specifications in the hope of getting the ensuing work, and in fact this can be a great way to find someone good who you have directly experienced you can work well with.

> " *I get tired of having to know what I want. Often I don't. So I posted asking for someone who was a WordPress expert and social media advisor and asked applicants to suggest what I needed done to my site before we started.* "
>
> **Sarah Wilson**, Australian TV presenter

Setting fee levels

Some of the marketplaces, especially for fixed fees, require you to give an idea of the budget for the project. You should have an idea of this in any case before you hire somebody. The primary reference points for fee levels should be the value to you and usual pricing on service marketplaces rather than the costs of traditional outsourcing or service providers.

Setting the target cost	
Assess project value to you	Make a realistic assessment of the value of the project to you based on the overall impact on your business. This is not always easy for projects with intangible benefits, however it helps to keep expected fee levels in perspective.
Research fees for similar work	Get an idea for what the market is paying by looking at fee levels for similar work on the service marketplaces.
Set a range you can afford	Based on the value to you and market rates you should set an overall budget range for the project. This will probably be as a fixed fee, however based on the estimated hours for the project you can also calculate a range for hourly rates. Be prepared to adjust your range if the bids you get suggest your range is unrealistic.
Account for transaction costs	Account for your own time that you might need to spend running the project, as well as any assistance you might require, which may be higher than using other channels. This gives you a view of the total costs of getting the work done.
Set contingency	Things can go wrong so set aside some money in your budget in case the project runs over or you have to hire help to sort out any problems.

Select hourly or fixed fees

Jobs can be done on a fixed fee basis, in which an agreed fee is paid for defined outcomes, or on an hourly rate. In the case of hourly pay, marketplaces provide mechanisms for logging hours worked, sometimes supported by monitoring the provider's computer so their work activities can be viewed by the client. Fixed fee and hourly rates are each relevant in different situations, so consider your situation and which approach is going to be most appropriate for the project.

Hourly fees versus fixed fees

	HOURLY FEES	FIXED FEES
Defined scope	If the task is clearly defined.	If the task is difficult to define or the cost of doing so is high relative to the value of the task.
Ongoing work	If you are looking for a worker for ongoing activities.	If you are looking for only a single defined task.
Defined value	If the value of the work is less clearly defined.	If the value of the work is clearly defined, enabling a fixed priced offer and selection of the best bids.
Ongoing relationship	Easier to develop an ongoing relationship.	Specific effort is required to extend the relationship.
Monitoring	Need to check what is billed.	Harder to see project progress.
Concerns	Provider could spend more time than is necessary.	Provider could take shortcuts or not focus on quality in creating the deliverable.
Control mechanism	Maximum hours in any given period can be capped, and work diary can be monitored.	Release of fees can be staggered based on reaching various milestones.
Disengaging early	Easy to disengage.	Harder to disengage before project completion, though setting clear milestones helps.

Finding talent

12

> *If I don't believe in you and trust you to begin with then I shouldn't hire you. And that's why I personally interview all the people we bring in here.*
>
> **Jerry Macnamara**, Internet entrepreneur

You want to find the best and most relevant providers to work on your projects. There are some great providers available, so your challenge is to ensure that you get the best talent to apply, and are able to identify who is likely to do the best work for you.

Chapter overview

- Filter the initial round of candidates to a manageable number and also invite additional interesting candidates who may not have seen the job.

- Interviews are very useful in assessing candidates for any significant projects, particularly in assessing how well you can communicate with them.

- Criteria to consider includes experience, specialist skills, communication capabilities, availability, and quality of work.

- Trial tasks and competitions can be a good way of assessing providers' capabilities before more extended engagements.

CASE
STUDY

How Kim "found the right guy for the job" on Elance

"I needed some help with WordPress blog stats, website crop navigation and PDF to HTML conversion. I posted the job on Elance and within an hour I had an offer. I was so excited that I actually got a bid, that I awarded the project immediately.

What I learned: *The project objectives and time line should be completely clear before awarding the project.*

What I wish I had known: *I wish I had used milestones to not only fund the project, but to make sure the guidelines were followed. Also, I realized after the fact that correspondence should always go through the Elance private message boards and not my own email or phone to protect myself from he said/she said problems.*

Outcomes: *Often I found myself repeating the objectives of the project. The Elance worker began wanting to be paid even though silly mistakes had been made and not corrected. I found myself wondering why the quality of what the Elance worker did was so poor. Then I figured it out. I pay him, he pays workers a fraction of it to actually do the work. This one just didn't work out. I had to pull the project and re-Elance it.*

I received multiple responses and this time I basically interviewed of all of them. In the end I found the right guy for the job.

What I learned: *If you spend the time before the job is awarded making sure the objectives are understood, then you're chances of a better experience increase drastically.*

Outcomes: *Perfection and delivered on time. He's respectful, honest, hard working and only delivers a polished final product. No sneak, sneaky.*

So, what has Elance done for me? My blog stats are fixed, the beautiful crop navigation on my blog is complete and of course, my PDF to HTML conversion is beautiful! I love to give recommendations, so please use my Elancer, Bhupendra Singh Kunwar."

Kimberley Murgatroyd, Jet Set Life

Select candidates

The number and quality of candidates for jobs that you post will vary widely. Jobs requiring highly specialized skills attract fewer candidates, however there are many domains in which there are broad pools of providers eager for work.

The process of filtering applications is fairly straightforward if there aren't many candidates, however if there are too many applications it can become tedious going through them all. You need to take a structured approach to evaluate applications efficiently, in a way that readily identifies the most relevant providers.

Filter candidates

The first stage is simply going through all applications to select those who are viable candidates. Depending on how many applications you have received, you will need to vary how stringent your criteria are. If you have many excellent candidates then the task in the first stage is to narrow the pool to a manageable number, certainly fewer than 10.

If there are only a few decent candidates then you will need to find anyone in the list who is worth considering in more detail.

If you only have a simple, clearly-defined task to get done, you don't necessarily need to go through the full list of applicants, just find one person who fits the requirements and seems capable and immediately award the job. Doing a more thorough analysis would be a waste of time given the task scope.

If it is a more challenging task, and no-one seems to fit what you are looking for, then don't hire anyone. Many of the platforms show candidates the proportion of jobs you have advertised that you have actually hired someone for, as they don't want to waste their time bidding if no work is likely to eventuate. But this is not an issue if you hire people for most jobs, and in the vast majority of cases there will be someone worth hiring.

Invite candidates

It is usually worth browsing provider profiles and inviting the best ones to bid for the job. Most of the major service marketplaces have this facility and it can be flattering to a provider that you have singled them out. There are some providers who are so successful that they only react to invitations and don't bid specifically on work, though the busiest providers will only respond to compelling opportunities.

Consider individuals versus teams

You can hire both teams and individuals on service marketplaces. There are advantages and disadvantages to each. There is no real advantage to hiring a team to do a simple task. But for more complex long-term projects hiring a team gives you access to a wider selection of complementary skills, which will usually include the project management role. They may also be able to deliver a quicker turnaround than solo freelancers.

One disadvantage is that the turnover within teams who use oDesk and Elance can be very high so you may find that the excellent developer you started off working with has been replaced by someone less gifted with little knowledge of what has gone before. It can also be hard to build relationships directly with the best individual providers, as the relationship is at the team or corporate level.

In general, if you need specialist work and have a very clear understanding of what you want, you will want to build relationships with talented individuals. If you need more assistance with project management you may prefer working with a team, particularly as they often have dedicated client relationship staff with good communication skills who can liaise with the specialists.

Interviewing candidates

Once you have a filtered group of candidates for a significant project you can consider them in more detail and then select around two to four for interviews. For clearly-defined tasks where there is an obvious candidate, it is still often worth interviewing them to check there is a real person behind the application, see that they can communicate effectively with you, and confirm they have availability to do the job in the timeframe you require. If things don't work out in the interview, which can happen, you can always interview others.

For larger projects it is almost always worth interviewing candidates. In an interview you will get to know them far better than through email, and it's also a great starting point to build a positive relationship with the provider.

For small one-off and well-defined tasks such as creating scripts for a website, and where there is no intention of repeat work, there may be no need for an interview.

Voice and text interviews

Whether you use voice or text chat for an interview will depend on the type of work and the provider. For more complex tasks or larger projects it is often good to use voice to interview a provider. Using Skype or the voice or video communication function within the service marketplace, if available, usually allows you to get the best sense of whether you and the provider can communicate effectively and will be able to interact successfully. If the provider's spoken language skills are reasonably good, this is often the most efficient way to communicate.

Some providers who are not native speakers are far more confident in their writing rather than their speaking and may prefer a text-based interview. They also may not have headphones or the necessary bandwidth, or sometimes are taking time during their day job, so cannot use voice communication. If roles require written language skills, then conducting an interview via text (instant messaging or email) is a good way to assess their ability.

If you are likely to use text or chat to communicate during the project then that is probably the best way to interview. One of the major advantages of using chat throughout a project is that you can later check back on what was discussed. This doesn't mean there won't be miscommunication, but it is minimized and far easier to identify later.

> *We look at freelancers' body of work, how much have they worked, their reputation, feedback received, and how much repeat business they have got. Our aim is to create long-term partnerships, not to keep tendering for new partners for every job.*
>
> **Davy Adams**, Managing Director, IDG Australia

Hire your provider

There are many criteria that you need to consider when selecting who to interview and finally who to hire. These fall broadly into the following areas:

- Experience
- Specialist skills
- Communication skills
- Availability
- Attitude and commitment
- Quality of work
- Practicalities
- Fees

There is a wealth of information available on service marketplaces to help you make your decision, including providers' profile, their work records, feedback, and of course your own experiences in interviewing them.

Experience

You will certainly want a good level of experience from your provider, but it doesn't always guarantee quality. Sometimes it's worth taking a chance on somebody less experienced who could still produce excellent results. Remember that experience is not confined to the record of work that has been carried out on the platform. They may have great experience from previous work or other service marketplaces.

Experience indicators	
Profile	The provider's profile should indicate and highlight important experience.
Cover letter	The cover letter to the application should provide specifics on experience relevant to your job.
Previous work completed	Check what kind of work the provider has been doing on the marketplace and how relevant it is to your project.
Total hours worked	This can be a better indicator of experience than number of projects as some individual projects or contracts may be large or ongoing.
Interview	The interview provides a chance to dig deeper into a provider's past work history.
Website and social media	A provider's website and social media profile (such as LinkedIn) will also indicate their work experience, though this may not be reliable.

Specialist skills

One of the most valuable uses for service marketplaces is to draw on specialist skills. Providers' skill levels should be apparent from their past work record and examples in their portfolio. They may also have specific work-related qualifications.

Specialist skill indicators	
Marketplace tests	The larger platforms have marketplace tests which reflect skill levels of providers, for example in specific areas of IT. These are a good way to check skill levels relative to other providers. As in the real world, test scores are not always the best measure of talent, but they can be a very useful indicator.
Education	Usually a provider will show any degrees or professional qualifications they have. You can check the quality of the educational institution and degree through search. Be aware that these qualifications are claimed by the provider and not checked by the marketplace.
Interview	Ideally you will be able to ask technical questions to assess their experience and understanding relevant to the task. Alternatively you can ask them to perform simple tasks, such as create a headline for a blog post, that will indicate their calibre.

Communication skills

Communication skills are important to working successfully together, especially when employer and provider are in separate locations. This is especially true if either of you are communicating in a language that is not your native tongue. It is critical to ensure you can interact successfully.

Communication skills indicators

Cover letter	If you have asked specific questions in your job description and these aren't addressed adequately then you should reject the candidate.
Interaction	Interacting before a live interview by asking specific questions provides a good indication of written communication, and whether the provider can understand your instructions.
Interview	Whether text or voice-based, the interview will give you the best indication of whether you can communicate clearly on a day to day basis.
Marketplace tests	The service marketplaces usually have an English language test and many providers take this to verify their communication skills.

Availability

Availability of providers is a major issue for clients and for the providers themselves. Providers sometimes over-commit by taking on too many projects, meaning that they are not able to deliver on schedule. You need to be clear on how much work will be required, your deadlines, and get clarity from providers that they will have sufficient availability to get the job done.

Availability indicators

Interview	Ask during the interview about their current work commitments both in projects already underway, planned for the future, or for ad hoc work which is likely to arise from an existing client relationship. You will also want to know whether they have full-time work, education, or other commitments in addition to their freelancing activities.
Feedback comments	Check if there have been any negative feedback comments from previous clients relating to availability or late delivery. If there is only one isolated example ask about it at the interview as there may be a valid explanation.

continued on the next page >

Availability indicators (continued)

Current workload

Check how many current projects they have running on the marketplace, and also whether they have consistent clients. If they are in strong demand and have good client relationships that is a good sign, but it may mean they are overcommitted. Be aware that a listed current project does not mean it is active, as clients can let work lapse. The most active providers like to close out jobs if they are not active, as the most demanding clients with large projects do not like their providers having other active jobs.

Quality of work

The single best indicator of the quality of a provider's work is feedback from other employers. Feedback is covered in more detail in Chapter 15 on Closing out. Looking at a provider's portfolio is also a great opportunity to assess quality.

Quality of work indicators

Feedback ratings

Feedback scores, both overall and on individual projects, give you an indication of the quality of a provider. Depending on your requirements, you might have a feedback cut-off of least 4.5, or even 4.9 out of 5. The higher your cut-off the more likely you are to eliminate highly talented providers who may have had an unfortunate client experience. Isolated negative ratings have to be taken in context so make sure you view both sides of the feedback associated with the comment, or ask the provider directly.

Feedback comments

Text comments in feedback can indicate outstanding quality of work and give context for negative ratings.

Number of feedbacks received

If there are only two or three feedback scores received be wary about using the overall feedback rating as an accurate indicator of quality.

Work samples

Most marketplaces allow providers to post samples of their work from their portfolio, or you can ask for relevant samples. These can be very useful, though be aware that it is possible the provider hasn't done all or even any of the work on the samples submitted.

Commitment and attitude

Judging commitment and attitude of a provider is subjective, but it is very important to anticipate the level of service you may get, as well as the potential for a long term working relationship. If you think there is the potential for an ongoing relationship, you will want to see how well you and the provider can communicate, what interests them in working for you, and sometimes their personal objectives.

Commitment and attitude indicators

Response times	How quickly you get responses from providers is a useful sign of their interest in the project, as well as a leading indicator of their responsiveness going forward.
Cover letter	The cover letter should indicate what motivates providers and some of their drivers for wanting to work on your project. The more targeted the cover letter the more time they have spent on it, which is another good indicator that the provider specifically wants your work
Feedback comments	Feedback comments from other clients will indicate levels of client service and may highlight examples of 'going the extra mile'.
Interview	The interview is the best place to get to know the provider so for bigger projects or if you are looking to build a relationship you can ask about issues such as their career objectives and what attracts them to the work you are offering.
Off-marketplace reputation	Client testimonials, reviews, and recommendations may be highlighted on the provider's website or professional social media profile. An online search may also uncover feedback from other sources.
Last worked	When the provider last worked on the platform can be an indication of their commitment to working as a freelancer. If there are many gaps in their work record ask about it during the interview
Total hours and fees worked	A high number of hours and fees worked shows a commitment to providing good service as a freelancer.
Work record	Repeat or consistent work for the same clients shows they are able to build good long-term working relationships.
Subcontracting	At the interview you should check with the provider, particularly if they are a team, whether they will be doing any subcontracting. It is important that they are transparent about this because any subcontracting arrangements means you potentially lack control over the results and you may need to get a Non-Disclosure Agreement.

Do the same things you would do offline — you're still going to interview, still going to get references and still going to ask for samples of work. Treat it like the real world because it is — it just happens to be remote and online.

Gary Swart, CEO, oDesk

Practicalities

There are various practicalities which may rule out some candidates. One employer decided he couldn't hire an otherwise excellent provider because she wasn't on Skype and had intermittent broadband access, which would have made communication difficult. Check out these kind of issues at the interview stage or through interaction beforehand.

Practicalities	
Time zones	Make sure that you are going to be able to find a time that suits both of you for regular check-ins, if that is required for the work.
Tools and connectivity	Make sure that the provider has all the tools, compatible software, and levels of connectivity required to perform the work you require.

Fees

Fees should never be the primary factor for choosing a provider. You will already have a good idea of what you are prepared to pay when you post the project. The best providers will often cost substantially more than those who are less good, but the difference in fees is usually warranted. This topic is covered in more detail in Chapter 11 on Specifying and Chapter 14 on Rewarding.

Trial tasks and competitions

You can see which candidates shine by giving them a smaller task to begin. This can provide a starting point to working on a bigger project or an ongoing relationship. It also reduces the risk of things going wrong. Once you are confident in their skills and have established trust, you can offer them larger projects.

On service marketplaces trialling tasks is common practice and many providers may well expect it, particularly if a potential long-term working relationship is mentioned in the original job specification.

Setting up trial tasks

There are a variety of approaches to setting up trial tasks and assessing providers' capabilities before you embark on larger projects with them.

Mini competitions

Select a number of stand-alone small tasks, either with a small fixed reward e.g. $50, or with the price bid by the provider, and choose a number of bidders to do the same task. This creates an effective competition in which you can find the best provider for the task, and attract the most talented participants by paying for their time.

Individual tasks

Break down a larger project into smaller tasks, and in the initial round select providers to work on each of these individually. Based on the quality of their work, you can use the best one or more providers to complete the work. If some of the work done by the other providers isn't up to standard you can have it redone by the best providers.

Using this method also helps expose those providers who might not be serious about the work. It is common for not all candidates to complete a trial task.

Use competition platforms

Competition platforms (see Chapter 21 for more detail) are dedicated to running competitions for tasks such as design, writing, or video production. These can be excellent places to uncover providers you would like to work with on an ongoing basis. Of course only do this if you have a task you would like to run on a competition platform in the first instance. The bonus may be finding someone outstanding for ongoing tasks without having to go through the competition process for every job.

Setting frameworks

13

> Split work into granular milestones. Instead of agreeing on paying $1,000 for a logo, split payments into $100 units, all linked to deliverables. For example, pay $100 after first sketches are submitted. This gives you the ability to get out of the contract if it turns out that the worker you got doesn't fit.
>
> **Andrei Railean**, Online entrepreneur, Andrei.MD

Setting clear frameworks right at the beginning on various aspects of a project is helpful for both employers and providers. This simultaneously enhances communication and minimizes risk, creating a better experience for both sides, superior outcomes, as well as helping to build relationships.

Chapter overview

- Breaking projects into milestones helps for many processes including quality monitoring and payment release.

- By establishing agreements upfront you can avoid many potential misunderstandings.

- By establishing a framework for clear communication you can maximize the chances of the results you want.

- Monitor the performance of providers throughout the project.

- Set in place other simple safeguards such as securing passwords to minimize the impact of anything going wrong.

How Strategic Government Resources set frameworks around a project

Ron Holifield is CEO and founder of Strategic Government Resources, a Texas-based firm that offers training and executive search services for local government, as well as operating the largest jobs board for government workers in the US.

Holifield used a service marketplace for a web based project. They needed "very explicit technical skills for a clearly defined end product." They got several applicants in who were interviewed on Skype by the Chief Operating Officer, and found a suitable provider based in India. They then structured the project so it went as smoothly as possible.

Holifield explains:

"The COO was actively involved in the project management. They actually put together a project management plan that the contractor reported back on a regular basis with milestones. And as they worked through it there were interactions back and forth. As he got to Point X, she would evaluate and say, "this isn't exactly where we're headed, can we tweak it a bit?" So it was a very interactive process. We also had an IT person to speak to them if necessary.

The contractor was paid on an hourly basis with an estimate of the total amount of time with some milestones and benchmarks for where we wanted to be and when, so it was not a fixed fee.

With the milestones we were able to be on top of the project with the presumption that ten days or so into the project we'd be able to pull the plug if it wasn't working. We structured the agreement so we had an "easy out" any point along the way if it just wasn't working how we wanted it to be.

I think that's probably a really important piece because it dramatically lowered the anxiety. We basically knew with weekly project meetings that at any given point we were only at risk of totally losing a week's worth of work. That gave us a comfort level to say "this is worth trying."

I feel like we got high value, we got good quality product and a good end result. It all worked very smoothly and there were no problems at all."

Setting milestones

Breaking a larger project into smaller projects or into a series of milestones is an excellent way to both plan and execute a project. Often the milestones will be fairly obvious. They may be points at which a review is needed to determine detailed requirements for the next stage of the project, or where there are critical dependencies that require input from other parties.

Break the project into milestones

Having smaller achievable milestones is much easier to plan around. This provides more points at which you can disengage if you need to, or you can bring in additional skills. It also is a good way to focus individuals and teams on the task in hand, although they also need to keep aware of the overall project outcomes.

Establish deliverables at each milestone

For each milestone establish a well-defined deliverable to ensure progress and to monitor quality. These should be easy to check, for example a draft structure of a report or the wireframes for a website.

Allocate payments to milestones

To minimize risk you can allocate fees up to each milestone. For hourly jobs you can allocate a maximum number of hours that can be done in a given period. For fixed fees you can release funds at different stages on the condition that the deliverable arrives by the due date.

Of course there are circumstances that might be beyond the control of the provider in creating delays so discretion and common sense always need to be in operation.

Establishing agreements

Documenting all major aspects of the work at the beginning of the project can help avoid misunderstandings and reduce the impact of any issues that may arise later.

Document milestones and project plans

Make the agreed milestones completely clear. Include these in a project plan to which the provider agrees. This should include criteria such as deliverables and any linked conditions of payment. There's no need to document everything, just the important elements.

Contracts and 'work for hire'

The default contracts entered into on the service marketplace by providers and clients are sufficient for most purposes. In some cases, particularly if you are building a company in which you may want to raise external capital, it may be worth establishing an additional direct contract with the provider that spells out that the relationship is one of 'work for hire', in which the client owns all rights to the outputs from the project.

Dealing with subcontractors

There are some providers on service marketplaces that may claim to be working on a project but will then subcontract the work. Particularly if you are working with a team, it is worth checking if this is happening. Although a sub-contracting arrangement is sometimes acceptable, it can also lead to issues on quality and also risk, if your project is confidential.

Non-Disclosure Agreements

In the business world in general, Non-Disclosure Agreements (NDAs) are over-rated. The real protection they provide is minimal. However by all means establish NDAs with providers if there is a good reason to do so. Some larger organizations will need to use NDAs to meet internal processes, and they can be important for startups where potential investors' due-diligence processes may look for NDAs to be in place with all service providers. If there is a sub-contracting arrangement you will also need to get the sub-contractor to complete one, or ensure their contract provides adequate protection.

The downside of NDAs is that in reality they provide little legal or real protection, especially across national boundaries. In some cases they can put off providers on small projects as it adds administrative time and cost. However most providers are used to approving client NDAs.

Document communications to reduce risk

As you go on with the project it is worth recording in writing:

- Any agreed milestones
- Any correspondence relating to a change in agreed milestones
- Anything to do with money or contracts
- Any discussion of problems that may result in disengaging

For these messages you should use in-platform email so these can be recorded, or use the official process suggested by the marketplace. This is important for dispute resolution processes, which are covered in more detail in Chapter 15 on Closing out.

Communicating clearly

Clear communication is essential to achieve the project outcomes you want with minimal risks. Here are a number of guidelines that will help to make sure that everyone has the same understanding.

Ensure clear communication

Choose communication channels	Select the most relevant communication channels for your primary communication. These might include voice, chat, email, video, or shared desktops.
Schedule regular communication	Select a diarized regular slot to discuss the project either with the provider or with your project manager, for example daily or weekly. If using a project manager there will probably be a similar arrangement between them and the provider.
Check for understanding	To ensure the provider understands, reiterate any agreements or decisions, or ask them to restate them. This is particularly important if either of you is using a second language to communicate.
Be responsive	Try to respond quickly to questions and let people know if you will be unavailable for a period. Often projects don't progress because providers need clarification on specific issues.
Ask for warnings about availability issues	Particularly for projects with a longer duration make sure you ask providers to give you information about any availability issues that may affect the project.
Set expectations for response times	For example, ask providers to at least acknowledge receipt of messages within 24 hours.
Put everything in writing	Following up verbal discussions with agreed points reduces risk and misunderstandings.
Ask providers for their opinion	Regularly ask providers for their input and opinion. Not only can you get great ideas, but it also builds relationships.
Keep providers in the loop	Keep providers informed about the bigger picture around the project and give them plenty of warning about any changes in circumstances such as changes of delivery date, potential changes in scope or need to increase or decrease the number of hours worked.

Monitoring performance

You need to monitor performance to ensure the job goes well. Do this in a structured, consistent, and transparent way. For larger projects you may well need to establish a quality control role. This topic is covered in more detail in Chapter 18 on Structures and roles.

Establish criteria

Establish the criteria for monitoring performance at the beginning of the project and ensure that this is understood. This may be around quality of output, for example you may expect there to be zero spelling or grammar mistakes in a report, or could be based on productivity, as measured by output in a given number of hours.

Monitor regularly

In the latter stages of a project when there is trust between the provider and employer it is tempting to relax processes for monitoring performance. Sometimes monitoring is left to close to the end of the process in reviewing the final deliverable. It is best to monitor consistently at regular intervals throughout a project lifecycle.

Use experts to check

You may need knowledgeable experts to check the performance on more technical jobs, such as software development. Given that checks should usually not take a long time to perform, you can often engage more experienced - and sometimes more costly - providers to do this.

Ask for context

Always ask for context from the provider when you believe there has been under-performance. Be mindful that providers are only human and there may be reasons why output has been below what you expect, or progress has been slow.

> ❝ *When I hire someone new, I give them a little test project on a backup server so they can't mess up any data, If it's obvious they're not the right person, you have lost very little.* ❞
>
> **Alex Auseklis**, VP Finance, Sundia Corporation

Other safeguards

There are a number of other safeguards that are sensible to follow through the course of a project to minimize the chances of problems. While it is unusual, disputes can arise with providers, and it is prudent to limit the impact individuals can have.

Avoid giving systems access

Don't give full systems access to providers you don't know. It's best to wait until you have built trust in them before allowing them to access important systems. Usually you can limit access to particular web domains or parts of the system. In larger organizations systems security can limit the work that can be done via service marketplaces, however usually code can be developed externally before being implemented on internal systems by staff experts.

Secure passwords

Make sure that providers access systems with their own logins and passwords that can be readily changed. Also try to ensure that they do not have access to your password systems.

Deactivate access when projects end

As a matter of course, make sure you deactivate access for providers to any systems after a project, as well as change any passwords or any other login details that might be known to providers. Even if you trust them as individuals, you do not want any more people than is necessary to be able to access your systems.

Ensure deliverables are correct

Before making a final payment make sure you have full access to any and all deliverables specified, and that they meet the required standards. If there is a dispute it means that the deliverables cannot be withheld.

Post jobs anonymously

It's important to remember that service marketplaces are open and transparent. If you post a project it is possible that you may be giving away information about your activities to your competitors. If this is the case you may wish to post projects in an account that does not reveal your company identity. Before you do this you should ensure you are not breaking any terms of use with the marketplace.

Rewarding

14

" External people are an extension of your core team. To build a network of trusted partners who will go the extra mile, give them latitude, pay them fairly and treat them with the same respect you'd give your internal staff. "

Davy Adams, Managing Director, IDG Australia

To attract and retain the best providers you need to reward them properly. But rewarding is not just about money. Working with the best clients and projects creates many non-financial rewards which can also be very important to providers.

Chapter overview

- You need to set reward structures prior to the start of the project and make sure these are clearly communicated.

- There are significant possible non-financial rewards for providers including good feedback, exposure, the guarantee of regular work, and flexible work.

- Consider developing and training providers to grow strong relationships and increase their value to you.

How Stef Gonzaga built up her business

Stef Gonzaga lives in Manila, Philippines where she works as a freelance web content editor and writer. She originally started out in 2008 writing a few articles for essays.ph, a web content house based in her home country.

She was promoted and the earnings helped her through her English major degree. After a year, having already built up some experience, she put her profile on oDesk, a process which she describes as "venturing towards a global market."

Although freelancing gave her financial independence from her parents, she also gets what she describes as "creative freedom, access to a lot of knowledge and time to spend with my family."

With some great feedback and examples of work online she already had a good reputation, which gave her a head start in finding work. As she found more projects she started to build up an increasingly impressive work record with clients from the U.S. and Europe, collecting feedback such as:

> **"** *I rarely give out 5-star reviews but this ODESK'er is a gem. A+++ Smart, meets deadlines. A real catch.* **"**

As the work increased, she was able to set the terms by which she worked and source higher paid projects. For example she refuses to write fresh samples of work, as there are already examples in her portfolio.

She started a blog aimed at the freelancing community in the Philippines, and was able to guest blog on some well-known freelancing websites. This not only gave her exposure but showed off her writing skills.

After three years Stef Gonzaga has a viable long-term business, a good client base and does something which she really loves. She is only 21.

Set reward structures

To attract and retain the best providers you need to reward them properly. Just as with in-house employees, pay levels are important, but not the only factor. By acting consistently you can increase your chances of securing the services of excellent talent, as well as keeping your project within budget.

Quality trumps cost

Fee levels charged by providers are generally a good, though not infallible, indicator of the quality of providers. When selecting a provider don't go for the cheapest option, as it may actually end up being more expensive if you have to hire somebody else because the work is not up to scratch. If you're paying hourly fees, then the higher productivity of more expensive workers may actually end up costing less than engaging someone on lower rates.

Research shows that the fees charged by the most talented people are reasonably similar between developed and developing countries. In these cases the primary value of a service marketplace is to find the best people to work with rather than necessarily paying less.

Set and communicate clear pay structures

For each project set out expected fees and pay rates, and also any potential bonuses linked to meeting specific milestones or outstanding performance. Communicate these clearly to all providers. Remember that provider pay levels may by default be visible to other team members in the team rooms on service marketplaces. You may wish to communicate reward structures and any changes to the whole team rather than individuals, if relevant.

Consider pay rises

For long-term projects, or if you have an ongoing relationship with a provider, you should consider pay rises if merited. If a relationship is important to you, you need to ensure that the person still wants to keep working for you, and places your work as a priority. If they are gaining experience and getting consistent quality work from other clients at a higher rate than you are paying, you may lose them as a provider. If you are paying more than others are paying them, you get loyalty and priority in doing your work on time, even with tight deadlines.

It is straightforward on all the service marketplaces to increase hourly rates or fees for defined pieces of work such as writing tasks. Changing fee structures can also be an opportunity to close the existing contract and give positive feedback to the provider before opening a new contract.

Award bonuses for great performance

Bonuses are rewards for outstanding efforts from individuals. They are a great way to build relationships and to recognize a provider's contributions, usually relating to exceptional quality of output or working extended hours. For example, if someone has stayed up all night to finish a job to meet your deadline, that should be recognized. Awarding bonuses can be conditional on reaching a milestone or a specific landmark, such as page views on a blog post, or they can be awarded retrospectively based on subjective assessment of performance. If a provider deserves a bonus, give it to them. You will be rewarded with loyalty, and the value of the bonus to the provider will very likely far outweigh its cost to you.

> ❝ *I can't buy lunch for someone sitting in Boston or the Philippines but I can give them a bonus and say I really appreciate your work, please go for lunch and have a beer on me. That's exactly the same way as I would interact if I was with someone here and say, let's go for a beer.* ❞
>
> **Jerry Macnamara**, Internet entrepreneur

Non-financial rewards

Fees charged on a project are far from the only thing that is important to freelancers. It is important to understand how you can reward them non-financially as well as financially, as this will help to attract the most talented and build long-term relationships with them.

Many non-financial rewards are about helping people who are making their living in a challenging way, by making life easier for them, and helping them to build their business and career. Think about how the best employers treat their staff and what they do for them other than pay their salaries. These are the kinds of things that attract the most talented providers.

Non-financial rewards for providers	
REWARDS	COMMENTS
Flexibility	Do not be any more strict on working hours, communication times, or deadlines than you have to. If you can allow work to fit around their existing commitments or lifestyle it is very attractive.
Consistent work	Irregular work is a challenge for providers. Consistent, predictable, and regular work that guarantees income is at a premium.
Interesting work	The best providers are highly intelligent and often more motivated by doing exciting, challenging projects than by money.

Continued on the next page >

Non-financial rewards for providers (continued)	
REWARDS	COMMENTS
Experience	Building specific experience and in particular a portfolio of work is an important part of newer providers establishing their career.
Learning	Developing skills through doing new types of work or specific education enables providers to expand their scope of work and to grow personally.
Reputation	There is little more valuable for a provider than excellent feedback scores and testimonials, especially when they are starting out.
Attribution	Giving credit to the provider on the work they help create can be valuable in building a portfolio and sometimes attracting new clients.
Referrals	Recommending excellent providers to your friends and personal network creates significant value for them as well as the freelancers.
Partnerships	Giving trusted partners the opportunity to participate in the upside of projects or initiatives will bring out the best.
Gifts	Gifts are a great way to let providers know they're doing a great job. Most will prefer financial rewards but small gifts, for example at Christmas or to reward exceptional effort, help cement relationships.
Social interaction	In some cases providers have limited opportunities for social interaction and will enjoy being part of a team and sometimes discussing topics other than work.
Pleasant working relationship	Positive, pleasant communication should be a given. The reality is if people enjoy working with you, you will attract and retain better workers.

Developing providers

Developing people is central to building long-term employment relationships within organizations, yet it is not often something that happens between employers and external providers. Just as talented staff will contribute more if they get training and education, and are more likely to leave if they don't, there is often real value to you in developing your freelancers. There are a number of approaches to developing the skills and capabilities of external providers, both formal and informal.

Give challenging work

For the best providers, give them work that is challenging and allows them to develop new skills. If this requires them to spend significant time studying to do the work, then agree on whether they charge for that. Often providers will be happy to spend their own time studying if they can then immediately apply their new skills on paid work, however within long-term relationships you should consider paying them to develop new skills if this will make them more valuable to you.

Promote trusted providers

Consider promoting trusted providers into project roles that require additional responsibility. These might include coordinating activity, project management, or carrying out quality control. The best source for these roles are existing providers who you know well. In some cases they may have been doing low-level work but demonstrated a thorough, reliable approach.

Give constructive feedback

You should always give constructive feedback. The scope of this doesn't necessarily have to be applicable only to your project. If there is feedback that may help the provider to win other clients or do better work for them, offer it. More obviously, make sure they know how you like things done. Feedback is usually best delivered on an ongoing basis as part of your normal communication process, but you can give it some structure, such as organizing point-by-point reviews or de-briefs after a project has ended.

Provide training

Training providers is often simply part of making them productive in the tasks they are performing for you, but can also be geared to help them develop marketable skills. Training can be provided by your staff, other providers in your team, or sometimes through online courses. You should certainly pay for any training, and if the skills relate directly to the work they are doing for you, for their time spent in training. This is a great way to develop relationships. You are investing in a person, and helping to develop their skills in a way that will benefit you too.

Be a mentor

If you have a very good working relationship with a provider it may be that you can give them advice or input on aspects of their business. This doesn't have to be a formal "mentor" relationship, but simply offering to act as a sounding board when they need input on a specific issue in their business.

Closing out

15

> *I brought on a graphic designer. It wasn't working out and I cut it quickly. That job was over in three days when it was a few weeks project. When it is obvious to me it isn't working out with something like that it's important to sever the ties very quickly. If you've made a poor hiring decision you need to move on quickly.*
>
> **Mike Todasco**, Founder, Sketch Maven

Finishing a project is an important part of the crowdsourcing process. Usually this will involve employers and providers sharing positive feedback about each other. Feedback is visible to all and a vital part of building online reputation. In some cases things don't work out and finishing a project may involve disengaging from a provider.

Chapter overview

- Feedback is the best indicator of provider and employer quality and should be taken seriously.

- Think carefully when you give feedback, and be generous where you can.

- If you need to disengage with a provider do it earlier rather than later.

- In the unlikely event of disputes, marketplaces provide structured approaches to resolving them, including arbitration.

CASE
STUDY

How one employer disengaged a provider before the job even started

A US-based clothes manufacturer used one of the service marketplaces to hire a provider on an hourly basis to "overhaul" their website. It was hoped that the arrangement would potentially be a long term one with ad hoc work continuing after the original project finished.

The employer was diligent in the hiring process. They got three good bids very quickly but one provider stood out for the employee. They were reasonably local (which was regarded as an advantage) and had some extremely good examples of work that could be shown, although they didn't have much feedback on the marketplace from previous projects. The provider was the most expensive, but the differential with the other two wasn't that much.

There was a fair amount of communication between provider and employer which was positive, with the provider being very responsive, so the provider was hired. The client sent off a standard NDA and other project documentation straight away as the project had an immediate start. The NDA was important from the client's perspective as there were some confidential elements to the project and had been mentioned in the original task description on the marketplace.

The client waited four days to receive a response from the provider and didn't receive anything so started to get nervous. Instinctively things didn't feel right and they took this as a strong indication of the provider's responsiveness. Based on advice from the marketplace itself they took the decision to disengage early so they cancelled the contract and awarded the contract to the second choice bidder, who had good feedback.

The result was that the second provider returned the NDA in an hour, had already produced good results by the next morning, and ultimately has proved successful.

The disengaging was done early and also gracefully. The client was contacted by the original provider who wanted to come and meet them to explain the situation, although this request was politely declined. In future the client says that they will take feedback and also marketplace tests as more important criteria in selecting candidates.

About feedback

On service marketplaces employers hire providers they will probably never meet. While the amount of money at risk is usually fairly low, choosing the wrong provider can throw a spanner in the works.

The single best indicator anybody has for successfully selecting a provider is the feedback ratings they have received from previous employers. Similarly providers also rate employers, and the best providers use feedback in the same way to check out the quality of the employers before applying for their projects.

You should take giving and receiving feedback seriously. It can affect people's livelihoods, and your own success in using platforms.

How feedback works

1 The feedback process usually starts when a job or contract on a service marketplace ends. This may also happen at certain milestones within a larger project.

2 You will receive a notification from the marketplace that a contract has ended, with a request to complete feedback on the marketplace website.

3 The provider will receive a similar email inviting them to give feedback, either at the same time or after you have given yours.

4 Both employer and provider complete and submit the feedback form.

5 Once both are complete, the feedback is visible to each of you and to other users of the marketplace.

6 If the feedback is negative you usually have a right to reply by adding a comment.

7 The feedback scores are aggregated into an average score for the provider and employer. In some cases individual project scores are weighted based on the project size, so a large project has more influence on the overall average feedback score than a small project.

Feedback types

FEEDBACK TYPE	COMMENTS
Overall project rating	This is a score, usually out of five, in which you rate the overall performance of the provider. On some platforms this is an aggregated score based on your ratings of different aspects of the project.
Detailed project ratings	On some platforms employers can score specific aspects of a provider's work. These include issues such as expertise, communication skills, and timeliness.
Milestone rating	Some platforms also allow you to carry out ratings at milestones in the project.
Comment	You can add comments about the provider's performance which offer praise, give more detail, or explain the context for ratings given.

Reading between the lines

It is important to look at the number of feedback scores received as well as the average feedback score. For example, an average feedback rating of 4.8 out of 5 from 20 clients is better than 5 out of 5 from 1 client, as it shows consistent good performance across circumstances and clients. Repeat work and feedback from a single client is an indicator of strong relationships.

Negative feedback suggest there may be issues with a provider. However if there anomalies, such as a single negative feedback among generally positive feedback, there may have been particular circumstances in one project. Be aware that some clients will unfairly give highly negative feedback. If there were problems try to assess the comments from each side to get a feeling for who is being reasonable and unreasonable. If there is plenty of very positive feedback, it is usually fair to ignore uncommon exceptions.

It is important to keep feedback in perspective. There are many clients who make a rule of never hiring providers who don't have a sufficient number of feedback ratings or a high enough average feedback score. This is a valid approach, however it does provide an opportunity for others to work with newcomers or those who want another chance to prove themselves, and often get exceptional service as a result. These providers will be particularly keen to earn top feedback ratings.

Giving and receiving feedback

When you're giving feedback carefully consider your ratings and any comments. Here are some things to bear in mind in both giving and receiving feedback.

Be generous

Absolutely, give five stars if you have had a great experience. Stand out providers usually have an average which is five or slightly below. In general you should give the benefit of any doubt. If things haven't worked out as you hoped, consider whether you may have contributed to the problems, or there are reasons the provider wasn't able to deliver. Don't give low ratings unless you are convinced they are deserved.

Explain negative feedback

If you had a really bad experience and are sure it was the fault of the provider, be it from their capabilities or their attitude, by all means give them a commensurate rating on the relevant criteria. If this is the case it is worth explaining any possible mitigating circumstances or relevant context in the comments.

Build relationships

If you want to continue working with a provider, you should support them how you can. That includes giving them highly positive feedback, which presumably they deserve if you want to work more with them. This is part of the non-financial benefits for the provider of working with you.

Discuss feedback

If you are going to give five star feedback, let the provider know. They are very likely to do the same for you.

Frequent feedback helps

Evidence of repeat work is great for providers, but this sometimes gets lost in very big projects or if work is ongoing. If you can break projects into smaller contracts, or end the contract and restart, this allows you to give feedback at regular intervals. Some platforms also allow for feedback at each milestone.

Your score is important

The best providers will look closely at the feedback employers have received before bidding on their projects, so take it seriously. Aim to make your providers think of you as a five star client.

Receiving poor feedback

If you do get negative feedback that you feel is unfair, then you should use your right to respond. Generally marketplaces will not remove feedback. You can approach the platform, but you are unlikely to get exceptions except in egregious cases.

Disengaging

Sometimes providers just don't work out and you need to end the project or relationship. The trick is to do it sooner rather than later. The more you have invested in a relationship the harder it is to pull out. You also want to avoid any situation where you are so far into a project that disengaging could cause the whole project to fail.

When to disengage	
Consistent low quality	Quality does not meet required levels.
Deadlines are not met	Agreed timelines for deliverables have passed without good reason.
Poor communication	You cannot communicate effectively with the provider.
Too much time taken	Too much of your time is being spent supervising or checking work.
Lack of trust	You believe the provider may not be acting honestly.
Lack of responsiveness	The provider does not respond to your communication for unexpectedly long periods.
Breaks contract	The provider is breaking the terms of the contract.

How to disengage

Disengaging is straightforward and it is sometimes a necessary step to finding the best talent. It's important not to lose sight that providers are human, and are doing their best to earn a living. There may be good reasons why things haven't worked out and by disengaging too early you may be missing out on working with someone who will bring real value to your business.

Check circumstances

Before taking action check any circumstance that might be causing the problem. Illness, family situations, or internet access being down may be valid reasons for lack of performance. Use your discretion in judging whether you believe these reasons are genuine.

Sometimes give the benefit of the doubt

You do not want unproductive relationships to drag on any longer than necessary, however there is a transaction cost in finding providers and building a working relationship with them. As such, you may choose to give the benefit of the doubt if you think they can come good.

Give a warning

If some aspects of the work are excellent but there are concerns then give a clear warning that you will end the relationship if things don't change. If applicable state this verbally, but also make your expectations clear in writing using the marketplace messaging system.

Disengage gracefully

If you do disengage then make sure you do it gracefully and professionally. If you have already given a warning then it should be clear why you have taken this action.

Give feedback

It's important to give honest feedback but do it with a cool head. If some of the work was good then say so. Strongly worded feedback may affect a provider's livelihood, but also may not reflect well on you. Some providers may get the impression that you are a difficult client to work for.

Disputes

In rare circumstances there are disputes between employers and providers. If you follow the guidelines described in earlier chapters these are very unlikely to occur, but it is useful to understand how to resolve disputes if they arise.

Types of disputes

Disputes are often about the quality or non-delivery of project deliverables or withholding of payment after work has been completed. They can also be about contractual issues including where the freelancer has provided work that infringes on others' intellectual property.

Resolving disputes

If you're clearly a victim of fraud or similar you should always speak to the service marketplace first. The service marketplace customer services will be able to help with instructions on what you need to do.

The usual next steps are a structured dispute resolution or arbitration process which is run through the service marketplace. They will usually go strictly by the small print of what is stipulated in their Terms of Use. If you have broken the rules in any way such as exchanging funds off the platform you are unlikely to get much help.

Some dispute resolution processes can only be applied to certain problems such as how payments have been handled, so arbitration will not always be an option.

Dispute resolution processes	
APPROACH	**HOW IT WORKS**
Facilitated dispute resolution	The marketplace will manage interaction between client and provider either electronically or on a call, on which they will be present. Funds may be held.
Marketplace arbitration	Arbitration usually follows if a first attempt at a mediated call fails. Both parties have to agree to the process. This involves submitting evidence about the dispute (usually in the form of records of communication about the work), and there is often an associated cost.
Third party arbitration	The arbitration may be outsourced via the platform to a recommended broker.

Keep records to support dispute resolution

Keeping records through the duration of a project is the best way to support any potential arbitration process. Unless you are corresponding about specific problems and a dispute is more likely, there is no need to go over the top on this. If you have broken the project down into milestones that are already on the marketplace then effectively the bulk of your agreement is already recorded.

Any output and any correspondence about the failure to deliver against milestones should be sent via the in-marketplace messaging system. Similarly any major points agreed verbally which aren't already covered in project milestones should be written and confirmed via email. This is good practice anyway to ensure there are no misunderstandings. Keeping these records on the system will be used as evidence in any arbitration process.

Service marketplace overview

16

> ❝ *The world is at the apex of an enormously creative and innovative shift that will result in profound changes to the everyday lives of people across the world.* ❞
>
> **Lynda Gratton**, Professor of Management Practice,
> London Business School

The service marketplace industry is well developed and growing very rapidly, with a small number of dominant players and a few other platforms that are succeeding by focusing on geographic or skill-based niches. As the marketplaces are all private companies we have to rely on their publicly provided data, which may not be directly comparable. However compiling what information we do have available helps to provide an overview of the industry.

Chapter overview

- The five largest general service marketplaces are Elance, Freelancer.com, Guru.com, oDesk, and vWorker.com.

- Employers are predominantly from U.S., U.K., Canada, and Australia, with freelancers most commonly in U.S., India, Philippines, and Pakistan.

- IT work is still the predominant category across most service marketplaces.

- There are a variety of other service marketplaces, some of them of a scale approaching those of the five largest platforms.

Major service marketplaces

	ELANCE	FREELANCER.COM
URL	www.elance.com	www.freelancer.com (and individual country sites such as www.freelancer.com.au)
Head Office	Mountain View, CA, U.S.	Sydney, Australia
Ownership / Funding	Privately owned, funding from Kleiner Perkins Caufield & Byers, NEA, FirstMark Capital, Stripes Group and other investors.	Privately owned, undisclosed funding from Startive Capital.
Founded	1999. Sold off enterprise business in 2006, and re-launched in 2007 as a web-based platform.	2004. Acquired and rebranded as Freelancer.com in 2009.
Total billings	$620 million	$150 million since payments were made mandatory through site (3.5 years)
Number of active project buyers	250,000	700,000
Number of active freelancers	2,000,000	3,600,000
Avg. projects posted monthly	75,000	70,000
Monthly unique visitors (Compete.com)	279,000	270,000
Alexa ranking	644	391
Top countries for freelancers (by projects, freelancers or hours)	By freelancers: 1. U.S. (36%) 2. India (17%) 3. Pakistan (6%)	By freelancers: 1. India (38%) 2. U.S. (15%) 3. Pakistan (11%)

		data as of end September 2012
GURU.COM	**ODESK**	**VWORKER.COM**
www.guru.com	www.odesk.com	www.vworker.com
Pittsburgh, PA, U.S.	Redwood City, CA, U.S.	Tampa, FL, U.S.
Privately owned, $500,000 from Fairview Funds in 2000.	Privately owned, three funding rounds 2006 -08 for total of $44 million from Globespan Capital, Benchmark Capital, T. Rowe Price and others.	Privately owned and funded.
1998. Branded as Guru.com in 2004.	2003	2001 as Rentacoder.com, rebranded as vWorker.com in 2010.
<No data>	$700 million (est.)	$93 million
<No data>	495,000	186,000
250,000	2,500,000	384,000
10,000	130,000	15,000
75,000	210,000	23,000
3,401	482	3,198
By freelancers: 1. U.S. (58%) 2. India (18%) 3. Canada (3%)	By payments: 1. India 2. Philippines 3. U.S.	By projects: 1. India (21%) 2. Pakistan (13%) 3. U.S. (10%)

continued on the next page >

Major service marketplaces (continued)

	ELANCE	FREELANCER.COM
Top countries for employers (by projects, employers or hours)	By employers: 1. U.S. (54%) 2. U.K. (8%) 3. Australia (7%)	By employers: 1. U.S. (24%) 2. U.K. (11%) 3. India (7%)
% of IT work vs. non-IT work (by earnings)	58%	81%
Commission	Service fee is deducted from freelancers: • 8.75% (standard service fee for relationships less than $10K • 6.75% (discounted service fee for relationships that exceed $10K and new referred relationships)	3% or 0% commission from employer, 10% or 5% or 3% commission from freelancer (lower fees with membership)
Number of tests / exams	450	186
Escrow available?	Yes	Yes
Dispute arbitration?	Yes Independent external arbitration also available for a fee,	Yes, for a fee of 5% or $5, whichever is higher (refunded to the winner of the dispute). Only for users who have elected to use the milestone payment system.
Worker PC monitoring software	Yes	No

		data as of end September 2012
GURU.COM	**ODESK**	**VWORKER.COM**
By employers: 1. U.S. (80%) 2. U.K. (6%) 3. Canada (4%)	By payments: 1. U.S. 2. Australia 3. Canada	By projects: 1. U.S. (47%) 2. U.K. (11%) 3. Canada (7%)
\<No data\>	59%	71%
Freelancers are charged 7.45% or 11.95% of an invoice depending on the freelancers status.	10%	6.5% to 15% commission paid by employee depending on the structure of the project (minimum fee is $3.00).
706	450	412
Yes	No	Yes
Yes, for a fee of 5% (minimum $25) deducted from the total amount in escrow. Only for escrow payments over $25.	Yes Only on hourly billings (not on quality of deliverables).	Yes, free to both parties. On all projects.
No	Yes	Yes

NOTE: User and activity data has been sourced from the companies and has not been verified. As presented, this may not provide an accurate view of the relative size and activity of the service marketplaces.

Other service marketplaces

There are a number of other service marketplaces of substantial scale not covered in the table. These include:

MARKETPLACE	NOTES
GetACoder	IT-focused marketplace.
GoFreelance	Encourages new freelancers.
iFreelance	Freelancers pay membership fees but there are no transaction fees.
JoomLancers	Focuses on Joomla developers.
LivePerson LiveExperts	Specializes in connecting consumers with experts for chat response.
PeoplePerHour.com	Initially focused on U.K. providers and clients, now global.
Project4Hire.com	Smaller general marketplace.
ScriptLance	Large IT-focused marketplace.
TaskArmy	Specializes in small well-defined tasks.
twago	Based in Germany, focuses on Central European market.
Witmart.com	English language sister website of Zhubajie.com (see below).
Zhubajie.com	Chinese language service marketplace with over 4.5 million users.

Microtasks are covered in Chapter 23.

PART V

MANAGING PROJECTS

17 Project management

18 Structures and roles

CROWD BUSINESS MODELS VII

USING OTHER PLATFORMS VII

CROWDFUNDING VI

MANAGING PROJECTS V

USING SERVICE MARKETPLACES IV

BUILDING RELATIONSHIPS III

APPLICATIONS OF CROWDSOURCING II

FUNDAMENTALS OF CROWDS I

Project management

17

> *Project management is the number one challenge of the entire crowdsourcing space. You can hire five hundred people at a time. How the hell do you manage them?*
>
> **Matt Barrie**, CEO, Freelancer.com

Project management is critical to successful crowdsourcing. While coordinating projects with providers scattered across different time zones has its challenges, there are a variety of tools, approaches and help available that can ensure things go as smoothly as possible.

Chapter overview

- Clearly defining the project with milestones, budgets, timelines, roles, outputs, and processes is central to successful project management.

- The right project manager with good skills and attitude can create substantial value.

- The service marketplaces each have a variety of tools that can help you manage your project.

- Many inexpensive web-based collaboration platforms are specifically designed to facilitate project management.

- Quality assurance is a critical part of project management of external workers.

CASE
STUDY

How Nick McMenemy runs virtual teams

Nick McMenemy is a serial entrepreneur who is now working on his third company, Virdium, which provides a cloud-hosted virtual desktop service. He relies heavily on crowds in building the company, and uses tight project management processes to manage them.

"'It is a most wickedly efficient way of working," says McMenemy. "I'm lean. By using this virtual team I can be like a multi-national 24/7." The initial business plan for Virdium had a cost of $250,000 for the first phase. It ended up costing $35,000 and being completed in half the time expected.

"The key thing is a very tight brief," notes McMenemy. "You provide a very granular approach to doing the task." He test the brief himself to check it is clear, and provides clear examples of what he is looking for as well as the process.

He sets benchmarks on successfully achieving work by time spent and failure rate, and specifies reporting formats and frequencies. This allows spot checks that work has been done correctly.

McMenemy has developed an Excel spreadsheet with pivot tables to summarize all information on work that is being performed. Increasingly he is automating the process by enabling online submission of work performed and reporting.

McMenemy wants IP ownership to be crystal clear. He had a lawyer draft a 2 paragraph clause saying any work done is 'work for hire', saying what he paid for that is "the best money I've ever spent." This must be printed out, signed, scanned, and sent before any work is performed. Payments must go to the same company that approves the agreement.

The first milestone is to accept the terms of service. A 50% payment is made as soon as any work is done. He then provides very detailed feedback, which can be 30-40 bullet points in clear English.

"Crowdsourcing means you can do a lot more for a lot less," says McMenemy. Effective project management of crowd workers is enabling his new startup to get out of the gates faster.

Establishing project management structures

As soon as companies go beyond using a couple of providers or outsourced crowd processes, project management structures are needed to manage the complexity. While there are many advantages to using crowds, it does require effective working and project structures. This should be considered a cost of using crowds relative to internal work. However often the project structures that are put in place for managing crowds can enhance the company's overall project management processes if these are not already fully developed.

There are many possible tools and platforms for project management, none of which is comprehensive, meaning that companies need to create their own solution using a set of tools that are comfortable and aligned with their current internal platforms.

A key criteria for project platforms is that they are easy to use by both internal and external staff. While some of the more sophisticated project management tools such as Microsoft Project can be very valuable in managing large projects, often simpler tools such as collaborative documents can allow team members to see what is going on and to keep tabs on their progress.

Project definition
A standard document should be developed allowing clear definition and communication of the project scope for all team members. Depending on the type of project, this is likely to include issues such as objectives, audience, timeframe, team members, budgets, and so on.

Milestones and metrics
As described in Chapters 11 and 13, setting and monitoring project milestones and success metrics is central to defining and achieving success from projects. Systems are required for monitoring metrics, including how they are gathered, update frequency, responsibilities, and where the information is kept.

Budgets
Budgets should identify expected costs on at least a weekly basis, and monitor actual costs against these. If you are using a single service marketplace, the use of project codes and reporting options usually allows this to be done fairly easily. If costs are incurred on more than one marketplace or from other sources, you will need a system to aggregate costs to ensure they are staying within budget.

Team members and activities
All members of the team, internal and external to the organization, should know who the other team members are and their respective responsibilities. This may be incorporated into

a project management system. Team activities may include regular calls or checks against progress, so team members are clearly aware of their communication responsibilities as well as the tasks they have been allocated.

Dashboards

Ideally managers will have access to a single dashboard that includes key indicators of project status for all of the projects they supervise, from which they can drill down to access more detail. It is possible to fully automate this, however it is not difficult to get microtask workers to assist in the data aggregation process.

Using marketplace tools

Service marketplaces have a variety of useful tools on the platform that are designed to help manage projects and processes with providers. These marketplace tools are useful but they are generally not complete alternatives to other platforms that are specifically designed for project and task management.

Communication

In-marketplace email is useful for any formal communications between employer and provider, ensuring that messages are on-the-record. Instant messaging or chat is usually available, and is particularly useful for larger teams who are all registered on the site. Some marketplaces are starting to add more sophisticated offerings, including video chat and desktop sharing.

Budget management

Dashboard views of accrued time and costs by project code are useful in monitoring costs and payments. Being able to set the maximum billable hours in any given time period also helps pay-per-hour projects stay on budget.

Monitoring tools

Some platforms have monitoring tools to ensure that providers are working during billable hours. This is done by recording screen shots of the provider's desktop and sometimes photos from their webcam which the employer can view. Agreeing to use these tools guarantees payment to the provider.

Using APIs

You can use the platform Application Programming Interface (API) to integrate your business processes or own project management tools into the marketplace, for example to create custom dashboards. There can be significant effort involved, but this will be worthwhile if you are an extensive user of the platforms.

Aggregator and value-add services

Some companies such as CrowdFlower and Data Discoverers provide services to help you manage complex crowdsourcing projects. These are focused on microtask-based projects, which often need specialist input, both in their design and in project management.

These aggregators add value in a number of different ways, acting as a layer on top of crowdsourced projects carried out on platforms such as Amazon Mechanical Turk.

How crowd process services add value	
Dashboards and interfaces	Dashboards allow users to view crucial data for project management, keep track of responses, and supply an interface to communicate with providers.
Consultancy	Input on project design, including advice on redundancy and checking data.
Project management resource	Experienced project managers to oversee and guide the whole process as required.

Using web-based project management tools

There are a wide variety of cloud-computing platforms that can be invaluable in managing complex projects, especially if your providers work across multiple locations and timezones.

Advantages of using workspaces	
Convenience	All the relevant project data and documents are in one convenient place.
Version control	Everybody can see the current and previous versions of documents used.
Spans timezones	Team members can access resources whenever required.
On the same page	All participants can see project progress, giving no ambiguity about deliverables, responsibilities, and timeframes.
Low cost	Project management workspaces are usually low cost, and some are even free.
Collaboration	Collaboration tools facilitate the work process.

Project management features

There are three primary areas in which cloud-based platforms can provide useful services for distributed project management.

Task management tools

Task and simple project management tools distribute tasks to nominated users, create to-do lists, manage timelines, provide Gantt charts, integrate with calendars, and usually provide email notifications on various criteria.

Document library

Document libraries are a central repository of relevant files providing structured folders, the ability to define editors and viewers, version control, and notification of changes by email. This can be provided by systems such as Dropbox or Box.net, or within project management spaces.

Collaboration tools

There are a plethora of very useful collaboration tools for distributed teams including chat, video, screen sharing, microblogs, and discussion forums. Real time document collaboration such as that available in Google Docs is especially useful for many kinds of projects.

Example of platforms

There are a range of well-established as well as newer platforms providing project and task management tools as well as various collaboration solutions. The market is maturing and products are evolving to provide a high level of sophistication and usability. Leading providers worth investigating include:

- Zoho (**www.zoho.com**)
- PBworks (**www.pbworks.com**)
- Google Docs (**docs.google.com**)
- Huddle (**www.huddle.com**)
- Basecamp **(www.basecamp.com)**
- Asana (**www.asana.com)**
- Smartsheet (**www.smartsheet.com**)

 Be a yardstick of quality. Some people aren't used to an environment where excellence is expected.

Steve Jobs, Co-Founder, Apple

Successful quality assurance

Quality assurance is a fundamental aspect of successfully managing crowdsourcing projects. You need to ensure that all output is regularly reviewed and that relevant standards are being met.

The first step is to define the success criteria for the project in terms of the quality of the end product. Some of these criteria will be objective, for example that certain levels of data accuracy are being met, that there are no spelling mistakes, or there is no evidence of plagiarism. Others may be more subjective, such as that design quality is excellent, or that work produced fits in with a corporate message or branding guidelines. Setting the criteria will help to define the process.

Define the process

Outputs	Define the outputs that need to be reviewed. These may be a document in progress, lines of code, prototype designs, or lines of data in a spreadsheet.
Measurements	Where possible define measures for what is acceptable. For example this could be bugs per 1,000 lines of code, scores of less than 12 on the Gunning Fog readability index for articles, 20 company contact details in an hour.
Subjective criteria	If criteria for quality is subjective consider who needs to be involved. Does a marketing person need to check against style guide or does the CTO need to review output?
Sample size	On data projects it often is not practical to review everything so use a common sense sample of work or results to review.
Review frequency	In larger projects you might want to do a regular check on all outputs. This might be daily, or less frequently if there are fewer changes or it is easy to fix mistakes.
Time frame	Set time frames and project stages for each major quality check required.
Reporting and workflow	Establish how the review outcomes will be reported, who will review them, and the quality control workflow.
Peg to milestones	Where possible match your quality control processes to your agreed project milestones.

Manage the quality process

Ensure you have the right tools to help you manage the process. Some of these might be about supplying the output, for example screen capture software to show user interfaces, while others might actually check the quality itself. For example for writing projects there are a variety of online tools that can measure word count, readability, potential grammatical errors, and check for plagiarism.

The quality assurance process should be documented for reference, and communicated effectively to the relevant providers and staff. Providers need to understand their roles and responsibilities in quality assurance, what will happen if standards are not met, and be comfortable that their work is valued within the required quality processes.

Projects that use microtasks may use specific techniques to ensure quality control. These are covered in Chapter 23 on Using microtask platforms.

Structures and roles

18

" *I have most of my team now reporting to one person who acts as a projects manager and understands the projects better even than me. I would like to get everyone reporting to them as soon as possible as there are always a stream of clarification questions to sort each day.*
Paul Madden, Managing Director, Automatica Ltd "

When organizations go beyond minimal use of crowdsourcing or external providers, it is important to build structures that enable this work to be performed efficiently and scaled where required. A key aspect of this is defining internal roles to manage the crowdsourcing process and identifying the right people for these roles.

Chapter overview

- Establishing crowdsourcing within large organizations requires a variety of roles including a business sponsor and a contractor manager.

- Specific process elements include setting relevant measures, defining approval processes, and creating approved provider lists.

- Capabilities can be developed through training and establishing ways to share lessons learnt.

- Specific skills are required by effective project managers and quality assurance.

CASE
STUDY

How eBay established a crowdsourcing program

Online marketplace eBay has major challenges in managing its catalogs, given the extraordinary amount of information they need to gather, analyze, and process. They used traditional outsourcing methods to carry out these processes but found costs were rising, and sometimes their existing suppliers couldn't meet eBay's demand for their services.

Ram Rampalli was a senior manager in the Selling & Catalogs team at eBay. He saw that crowdsourcing using a microtask platform was a potential alternative to outsourcing. After trialling the aggregator CrowdFlower he established a crowdsourcing Program.

Rampalli writes on the CrowdFlower blog:

"When I started the crowdsourcing program within my group, I was planning to implement one or two projects. Within weeks, the number of projects grew to six. In the last year, we have experimented over fifteen different types of projects.

As more and more projects with CrowdFlower graduate to production, different groups (engineering, product management, quality engineering) across the organization are seeing the benefits of crowdsourcing and are keen on embracing this new paradigm."

As the program started to pick up Rampalli was named by eBay as 'Crowdsourcing Evangelist', responsible for the strategy, roadmap, and implementation of crowdsourcing projects to help create a better experience for their customers.

Defining roles within the organization

As companies start to develop crowdsourcing capabilities and allocate internal responsibilities there are a number of roles at both organizational and project levels that can be valuable in establishing solid, useful structures.

There are varying degrees of centralization that can be applied to crowdsourcing processes, however there should always be one or more people who have overall responsibility for the organization's access to crowd work. They will establish guidelines and monitoring and reporting processes, and in some cases will be the primary contact point for external workers.

Internal roles

ROLE	LEVEL	RESPONSIBILITY
Business sponsor	Organization	Ultimate responsible for the activity within the organization. Should be champion at or to board or senior executive level. Where use of crowdsourcing is strategic, this must be a senior role.
Contractor manager	Organization	Responsible for operational crowdsourcing within the organization. They will manage the platforms, develop guidelines, and carry out management reporting.
Project manager	Project	Responsible for the successful completion of a project. They may be external depending on internal resourcing or the skills required.
Quality manager	Project	Ensure that the required standards are met throughout a project. They usually report into the project manager but may work across projects.
Local champions	Business units	They may be early adopters or particularly knowledgeable about crowdsourcing. Their role is to act as champions or change agents within business units of larger organizations.

> ❝ *I'm trying to embrace crowdsourcing as a core competency. Part of my job as CEO, is to really try to understand these processes.* ❞
>
> **Phil Sim**, CEO MediaConnect

Establishing structures

Once there is recognition of the value of building crowdsourcing capabilities and at least one role in the crowdsourcing function has been established, clear structures and processes need to be developed and implemented.

Time and effort will be required to embed crowdsourcing processes into an organization. As discussed in Chapter 9 on Changing organizations it may be useful to run accompanying change management initiatives. There are a number of steps required to build structures for crowdsourcing.

Consult stakeholders

Some functions, particularly in large organizations, may perceive crowdsourcing to be risky. In establishing any crowdsourcing structures you will probably need to touch base with the legal, risk, human resources, and procurement functions. Some of them may not support the crowdsourcing initiative, which points to the value of the business sponsor role discussed in the previous section. However they should all be able to provide useful input into effectively structuring the new function.

Identify existing users

Where possible identify who in the organization is already using crowdsourcing. An audit of existing usage allows this to be consolidated into the new processes. It also helps you to uncover potential champions who can provide input on good practices, educate others, and help evangelize use of the platforms.

Consolidate activity with platforms

If there are sporadic patterns of crowdsourcing, for example on different platforms, it will be worth consolidating and rationalizing use on a preferred platform or platforms with a centrally negotiated contract. This may lead to more favorable fees reflecting increased use. It also allows any internal standards and processes to be applied to all external work, as well as easy financial reporting.

> *We are seeing the emergence of a formal role of distributed work manager. When outsourcing became mainstream many companies established specific roles for outsourcing. With the rise of the virtual workplace, in some companies people are now being appointed to orchestrate resources inside and outside the organization.*
>
> **Fabio Rosati**, CEO, Elance

Develop processes

A central activity of any crowdsourcing function will be to develop guidelines and processes that support the successful use of crowdsourcing. There are a number of areas that need to be addressed.

Establish performance indicators and measures

Establishing Key Performance Indicators (KPIs) and measures on crowdsourcing projects should be done at both project and organizational levels. This enables senior management as well as the operational team to assess and improve performance.

Measures may include:

- Estimated cost savings against using in-house resources or traditional outsourcing
- Differences in quality against using in-house resources or traditional outsourcing
- Average turnaround times
- Feedback given to providers by internal staff

Create approved providers list

As you do more crowdsourcing it can be valuable to consolidate internal feedback with existing external feedback to create an approved providers list. Accompanying this will be a set of guidelines that helps an individual user to select the most relevant providers. This makes it easier for users, and helps to minimize risk.

Establishing an approved provider list can enable preferential terms from those freelancers, and in particular first call on their availability.

Standardize processes at a project level

Establishing standards or workflow processes for projects facilitates the effective use of crowdsourcing. In general the simpler and easier the processes, the better. Their primary intent should be to make it easier to use external providers, while ensuring that risks are well-managed. Example of processes may include:

- Approval for crowdsourced projects over a certain cost
- Use of templates for writing job descriptions
- Job postings to certain platforms only by authorized people
- Specific on-boarding processes for new providers such as NDAs, contracts, or other documentation
- Defined approaches and minimum quality standards

Develop capability

Once crowdsourcing practices are established it is important to continue to develop organizational capabilities. If the initiatives are initially successful their scope will expand, which will require more established processes and structures. Over time crowdsourcing capabilities can become central to an organization's competitive advantage.

Training

Establishing formal or informal training programs with related guidelines can be very useful in developing capabilities within the organization. These can be delivered in a range of formats, including running group or one-on-one training sessions, producing written and online training material, and providing guidelines for writing job specifications.

Learn from experience

Crowdsourcing is a fast moving field and it is likely that how organizations can gain the most benefit will change over time. Ensure that you are able to capture and apply any experience and lessons learned, and reflect this in your processes, guidelines, and training. Where relevant it is worth supporting a community of crowdsourcing users to share what they have learned, or otherwise build informal sharing of knowledge and experience.

Create enterprise solutions

Where crowdsourcing use expands significantly there may be a need for the crowdsourcing function to use or develop dedicated systems or interfaces. For example this could involve a predefined labor pool who have been vetted for a confidential project, or building an interface from business processes or your enterprise systems to the crowdsourcing platforms. Most of the major platforms have APIs that enable access to all parts of the provider management process. Some also are starting to build bespoke solutions in partnership with major clients.

Defining the project manager role

Projects usually involve multiple tasks and multiple providers. To achieve higher quality you need a greater degree of specialization. However this introduces complexity in having to supervise multiple providers and manage the interfaces and integration between their work.

The role of the project manager is to understand the big picture of the project and to manage all of the individual providers to create the desired outcomes within deadline.

Skills needed

Skills required depend on the type of project, but will include considerable experience with project management, excellent attention to detail, and outstanding communication skills for their dealings both internally and externally.

Specialist knowledge needed

In theory projects can be run by project managers without deep subject matter expertise, who can draw on specialists as required. In practice many projects, particularly smaller ones, will need a project manager who can deal knowledgeably with all team members.

Internal vs external

For complex projects where you need to regularly give your input, or where there are a significant number of internal stakeholders who need to be kept in the loop, there are substantial advantages in keeping the project manager role internal.

This may also be the case if the project is long and ongoing, or is likely to mutate into other projects, and you need to leverage the knowledge and experience gained as the project progresses.

However for more straightforward projects that don't involve large numbers of stakeholders it is feasible to have the project manager position external.

Using trusted providers

Using existing trusted providers as a project manager can be an excellent option. This not only builds relationships and means you are using somebody you trust, but they also will already be familiar with the processes you use and the kind of output you expect.

Project managers on service marketplaces

Another option is to engage a project manager on one of the service marketplaces. The advantage is that they will already know how the service marketplace works, and how to work effectively with other providers. Some of the marketplaces have recommended project management specialists who provide this service.

Defining the quality assurance role

Quality Assurance (QA) is a vital part of the effective use of crowdsourcing. Getting the right people for the job and defining their role well is fundamental to ensuring quality output and successful project outcomes.

Skills needed

Candidates for QA roles need to have extreme attention to detail, be very methodical, be able to follow processes, understand requirements for reporting, and have excellent communication skills.

Subject knowledge

As for project managers, in some cases, such as writing, coding, or user interfaces, the QA team members may need to have specialist subject knowledge. In addition data-driven projects may require experience of established QA methodologies such as sampling, using gold standards, and redundancy.

Internal vs external

There can be multiple layers of quality assurance. For example for large data-driven projects you may need two tiers of quality assurance, with the first tier's work being checked by more experienced staff. In this case the top layer of QA is likely to be internal, while lower levels of QA may be carried out by external providers. For smaller companies and simpler projects hiring an external QA manager may be attractive if there are resourcing issues. However it is likely you will need some internal QA person checking to ensure projects are meeting your internal standards.

As described in Chapter 25 on Crowd business models, one of the challenges and opportunities for companies using crowds extensively is to push QA out to the crowd in order to scale operations. However there are real limits on the degree to which that can be done for core processes.

Using trusted providers

As with project managers, existing providers who have established performance and trust provide an excellent pool for recruiting QA staff.

Cross-over with PM role

For smaller projects the project management and quality assurance roles can be carried out by the same person. This helps to limit resources required, however it can be useful to separate the roles, as one person is more far likely to overlook issues than two.

PART VI

CROWDFUNDING

CROWD BUSINESS MODELS — VIII

USING OTHER PLATFORMS — VII

CROWDFUNDING — VI

MANAGING PROJECTS — V

USING SERVICE MARKETPLACES — IV

BUILDING RELATIONSHIPS — III

APPLICATIONS OF CROWDSOURCING — II

FUNDAMENTALS OF CROWDS — I

Using crowdfunding platforms

19

> " *Our contributors on Kickstarter pledged money towards our goal with no guarantee that we would ever be successful. They took a leap of faith... The Glif is now a full-fledged crowd-funded product.* "
>
> **Thomas Gerhard** and **Dan Provost,**
> Designers of "The Glif" iPhone mini-tripod

Everybody loves the story of the ordinary guy who invents something brilliantly simple and goes on to become a millionaire. Crowdfunding provides an opportunity to participate in making those dreams reality, not only by accessing some of the funds required, but also through engaging with the crowd for valuable feedback to turn concepts into products.

Chapter overview

- Crowdfunding works best for well-developed creative projects from which funders can receive tangible benefits.

- The most successful crowdfunding projects showcase both the qualities of the incentive and the passion and enthusiasm of those behind the project.

- The crowdfunding process is an opportunity to engage with the crowd to receive feedback and create a community of potential customers and evangelists.

- Crowdfunding can be applied to a variety of endeavors including philanthropic funding.

How Lumi Co kick-started their dream business through crowdfunding

Lumi Co is a young innovative design and print start-up based in Los Angeles. Founded in 2009, Lumi has used crowdsourcing not only to fund its business but also to generate volumes of publicity, goodwill, and advice.

Jesse Genet, 22, has invented a new process that allows vivid imagery including photography to be printed on to most natural materials, including cotton, leather and silk.

Genet, working with a designer, Stéphan Angoulvant, 24, used the crowdfunding platform Kickstarter to ask for funds to start up their business.

They posted a video which demonstrated the strength of their product, showed their own passion and determination, and told their fascinating back story. Additional incentives were offered through a range of luxury products.

Genet and Angoulvant successfully connected with the crowd. Funders such as blogger Gianna D'Alerta admitted "their video did such a great job at doing their pitch, I thought what's 30 bucks, I get to help someone get closer to achieving their dreams."

Total pledges came to $13,598, exceeding the $12000 Genet and Angoulvant originally asked for. They also received high quality advice from other entrepreneurs which helped them to refine their product and approach.

They also created a community of potential buyers who wanted them to succeed. On top of this the media picked up on their story, resulting in an appearance in an article on the BBC website.

Angoulvant regards Kickstarter as "an incredible platform" and "a powerful tool to connect with a community passionate about our work, to help us collect critical insight, and to provide a time line that helps us organize our activities as we grow our project."

Fundamentals of crowdfunding

Crowdfunding is a way of funding projects by getting contributions from many funders, each of whom makes a usually small contribution. While it is not an entirely new model, the advent of the web has made it far easier to do. Over the last few years the model has grown dramatically, with now dozens of crowdfunding platforms around the world.

An early example of online crowdfunding was the U.K. band Marillion, which raised $60,000 on the Internet from fans to fund a U.S. tour in 1997. In 2000 ArtistShare became the first platform that allowed creative projects to be funded on the web. After IndieGoGo was set up in 2006 to facilitate the crowdfunding of films, the sector blossomed.

There are two types of crowdfunding that are fundamentally different: crowdfunding for equity, which is covered in detail in the following chapter, and crowdfunding in which funders receive no equity. Equity crowdfunding is becoming increasingly viable as models are developed that conform with the current strict securities regulations in developed countries, and legislation appears in some cases to be relaxing. However in most cases references to crowdfunding are to the 'traditional' model in which no equity is granted to those who fund projects.

Funders are usually offered incentives, such as a pre-release DVD or CD, a name on credits, or a meeting with the artists. In some cases the crowdfunding process is effectively a pre-sale of products that have not yet been created. More often funders are motivated more by contributing to something worthwhile rather than simply purchasing a product.

Most crowdfunding platforms require a pre-specified minimum funding level to be reached before the contributions are made. That funding amount is supposed to be sufficient to allow the project to happen, so people do not pay unless the project is fully funded and can proceed.

Types of project

Crowdfunding is most often used to fund artistic ventures that funders anywhere can readily experience, such as music, film, games, writing, design, fashion, and art installations. However there are many other types of projects to which crowdfunding has been applied, including products, communities, vlogs (video blogs), buildings, philanthropy, inventions, startups, and technology projects. There are no real constraints on what can be crowdfunded if you are able to attract contributors.

Incentives

Beyond the satisfaction of having funded a worthwhile endeavor, many funders look for more tangible outcomes, even if they are just personal evidence of their contributions. For creative projects this will usually include copies of any work produced, often in special editions or received before others. Another significant incentive for funders is public recognition in various formats.

Platforms

Some choose to crowdfund directly, creating a website and asking for contributions for their project. However there are now a wide variety of crowdfunding platforms that not only facilitate the logistics of accepting contributions from existing networks of contacts, but also give access to broader pools of people who are interested in participating in worthy projects. The platforms also allow funders to give feedback and conduct a dialogue with the project originators.

Other benefits

Crowdfunding is an excellent way to test concepts. If a project fails to produce the desired level of funding it is very direct feedback that the proposition needs to be changed or better communicated. Even when the required levels of funding are received, funders may provide critical feedback on the project or concept that allows it to be refined or improved.

Very importantly, crowdfunding also facilitates connecting with large crowds of potential future customers and brand ambassadors. For example, Iron Sky, a science fiction comedy predicated on Nazis returning from the moon in 2018, is crowdfunding €900,000 out of a total budget of €7.5 million, with the remainder coming from government-related film bodies. A major benefit of using crowdfunding for a relatively small proportion of the budget is that it is a very powerful way to build an interested and engaged community well before the film is launched.

Scoping projects

Crowdfunding is not appropriate for all projects and all people. There are a variety of factors to consider before taking the crowdfunding route. However if you are already committed to undertaking your planned project, there is usually little downside to trying. Here are some of the factors that should be in place before funding.

Critical elements for crowdfunding projects	
Creative	What you are doing should be new, innovative, creative, and make something that did not exist before.
Engaging	Ideas need to capture the imagination of a community of potential funders.
Incentives	You need to consider what incentives you can offer that will be attractive to potential funders, and which are commensurate with the usually small funding amounts you are likely to receive.
Viable	You need to be sure the project can be done and that there will be no unanticipated roadblocks. By accepting funding you are guaranteeing the project will be completed.

Continued on the next page >

Critical elements for crowdfunding projects (continued)	
Energy	Before you crowdfund, you also want to be sure that you have the time, energy, and resources required to complete the project. You are accepting what may be a major personal commitment.
Passion	To attract interest you need to be passionate about your project and its success, and able to communicate that effectively to others.
Intellectual property	In most cases there are not intellectual property issues from crowdfunding. However there can for example be issues with creating patentable inventions in a public space, so consider the legal implications of public crowdfunding of projects.

 There's something very potent about buying an exclusive product and feeling like you've put money directly into the creator's hands for something they really want to make; and as a creator or entrepreneur, the lack of middlemen and gatekeepers is just as exhilarating.

Adrian Hon, Founder and Chief Creative, Six to Start

Setting up a crowdfunding project

Setting up the project and posting your crowdfunding pitch is critical. This is your shop window to the world and it must resonate with the crowd to attract the funding it needs to succeed.

Select a platform

There are an increasing number of crowdfunding platforms available. Some of these, such as Kickstarter, cover all kinds of projects, while others are focused on particular niches, for example music projects on Sellaband. It's always worth reviewing a selection of projects on each site to see if there are any platforms that seem a good match with your project and approach. Also read the rules as some have particular guidelines about the types of projects that can go on to the site.

Since most crowdfunding is community based, a significant factor is the geographical reach of the crowdfunding platform. Many draw their funders largely from a single nation.

Decide level of funding and completion date

Carefully select the amount of funding you are seeking. It is important that the funds are sufficient for you to complete the project, because that is what you are committing to do. Scope the project well so you have a very good idea of the funding required. You do not want to ask for too much, as that decreases the chances of meeting your target. Give funders sufficient time to make their move and for you to spread word about your project.

Determine the incentives package

Put a lot of thought into your incentives package. You don't want the structure to be too complex, but the idea is to provide different rewards for each tier of funding you are asking for. For smaller contributions hopefully you can provide some form of the project's output to the funders. Funders who are contributing substantially more may expect something more personal, such as a personally autographed document, a meeting or video call, or a limited series edition. Recognition in the form of credits on the creative product is often seen as desirable, as reflected by Buyacredit.com, which explicitly funds films by selling an appearance on the film credits.

Tell your story

Your pitch should be as media-rich as possible, including descriptions, images, and quite possibly videos. The more tangible you can make the project and what the outcome will be, the more powerful the message. You are not only selling your project and its output, you are also selling yourself. People can engage just as much with the inventor as the invention. Get across your passion and authenticity.

> *We have spent time cultivating relationships with real people, so when we ask for contributions we get them.*
>
> **Venessa Miemis**, futurist, artist, and change agent

Collaborating with the crowd

Once your project is posted the remainder of the crowdfunding process is about interacting with the crowd. Your success in funding the project will hinge on how well you engage with and respond to potential funders.

Modify on the run

If a project looks like it won't hit the threshold funding level, the proposal can be altered. For example hip-hop legends Public Enemy used Sellaband to try and raise money to record a new album. An initial requested funding level of $250,000 proved to be too much, but a scaled-down version of $75,000 which included both recording and promotion resulted in them reaching their target.

Get input

Crowdfunding projects provide a valuable opportunity to get feedback on your product as well as real business advice. For example the founders of Lumi Co, the print and design start-up covered in the case study opening this chapter, received useful input not only on product design, but also on how they project managed their business operations.

Build communities

Engaging with the crowd of funders helps to build an army of customers and brand ambassadors. Try to make sure that this doesn't dissipate after the project closes. Find ways to continue to communicate with funders or those who considered funding, partly in priming them for other crowdfunded projects, but also to let them know about other activities and completed projects they may be interested in purchasing or supporting.

Learn from results

If your project doesn't receive the funding needed, consider what you have learned and what you might do the next time to increase your chances of success. If you did make your funding target, work out what you did well and could do better next time. It is possible that you will be able to draw on the same pool of funders, however you may need to broaden your reach to bring in new contributors.

Philanthropic crowdfunding

The principles of crowdfunding are admirably suited to philanthropy, in attracting sufficient funds from many contributors to achieve worthwhile objectives. Arguably almost all charitable organizations rely on crowdfunding in having many donors, however this has traditionally been done using a variety of direct marketing approaches. Crowdfunding techniques that take advantage of connectivity and how they bring together communities of donors help to build new opportunities for philanthropic funding.

Microfinance

One of the best known examples of philanthropic funding is the microfinance organization Kiva. Microfinance, which involves providing very small loans to individuals and businesses, usually in developing countries, has been building momentum over the last couple of decades to become a significant economic force in some nations. Kiva uses crowds to fund microfinance projects, in partnership with a variety of microfinancing organizations around the world. Donors can select the specific project or person they are funding and see the outcomes.

Fundraising platforms and aggregators

Fundraising platforms such as Crowdrise and Razoo enable any nonprofit organization to set up their own crowdfunding initiative. A fundamental aspect of these kinds of platforms is a social element that enables individual donors to connect with others and to bring their own personal networks into the fundraising process.

Other platforms such as Causes essentially act as a front-end for crowdfunding, where funders can allocate their funds to a wide variety of worthy causes. These can attract very large communities that encourage each other and build a deep funding pool. For example Causes' Campaign for Cancer Prevention has over 6 million members and has raised $400 million.

Equity crowdfunding

20

> Start-ups and small business will now have access to a big, new pool of potential investors — namely, the American people. For the first time, ordinary Americans will be able to go online and invest in entrepreneurs that they believe in.
>
> **U.S. President Barack Obama,** on signing JOBS Act

In an environment in which lenders are risk averse, investors are skeptical of investment advice, and 99% of business ideas go unfunded, crowdfunding has the potential to revolutionize capital raising. The U.S. JOBS Act will enable broad-based equity crowdfunding however is not yet in place. However in the U.S. and other countries there are a number of approaches and platforms that can already be used in certain situations.

Chapter overview

- Until recently legislation in most developed countries prevented privately held companies from selling equity or debt to the public

- In 2013 SEC rulings will be made to enable equity crowdfunding for small offerings under specific conditions

- The equity crowdfunding landscape in the U.S. and in other countries is expected to evolve rapidly but there are likely to be obstacles and setbacks

- There are currently three primary models that crowdfunding platforms use to fund for-profit business projects

- A company looking to employ crowdfunding should understand its advantages and disadvantages compared with other ways to raise capital

Crowdfunding as an investment opportunity – Trampoline Systems

One of the best-known examples of crowdfunding for investment purposes is at London-based technology company Trampoline Systems. Previously financed by a hedge fund, the "social analytics" company found itself in a quandary in 2009 as the global recession began to bite. Needing additional backing quickly, it turned to crowdfunding, seeking to raise £1 million from a maximum of 100 investors. They needed to work within the constraints of U.K.'s Financial Services Authority (FSA) regulations and did not want to go down other micro-financing routes that involved investing in a club or fund that would not provide real equity for investors. As such, the company decided to break their funding into three tranches.

The first tranche occurred in October 2009 for £250,000, offering a minimum stake of £10,000 for a 0.2% holding in the company. The response was enthusiastic with over £300,000 raised.

Trampoline Systems Chairman Charles Armstrong has written candidly about the problems with the regulatory environment around crowdfunding in the U.K. He believes that offering equity is the only way to "provide investors with strong enough assurance that they'll get a fair return at the end of the journey." However this can prove extremely difficult within the FSA regulations.

Despite these difficulties, the exercise has created both publicity and trust, resulting in angel investors and even venture capital funds with no previous connection to Trampoline approaching Armstrong. In November 2010 the company announced investments from what it referred to as ten "leading figures in the software and financial industries." Their model has been cited as evidence to a Parliamentary committee investigating new funding models for the arts in the U.K.

The state of equity crowdfunding

One of the key challenges for entrepreneurs and business owners is access to capital. Many business owners are unable to obtain funding from traditional investment sources and an estimated 99% of new business ideas go unfunded as a result. Obtaining many small investments through crowdfunding is potentially a powerful funding opportunity for the more promising of these businesses.

In most countries, unlisted private companies are unable to sell equity or debt to the public. This means that while companies are able to request money from the public, they are unable to offer shares or bonds in exchange for that funding.

However the landscape is rapidly changing, notably with the signing by President Obama of the U.S. Jumpstart Our Business Startups (JOBS) Act on April 5, 2012, which in certain situations exempts small offerings from the requirement to register with the Securities and Exchange Commission (SEC).

The SEC was given 270 days to provide specific rulings under which the Act will come into force. While SEC Chairman Mary Shapiro has said the equity crowdfunding rulings will be made by December 31, the pace of rulings so far suggests that won't be achieved.

A large number of companies are preparing to facilitate equity crowdfunding for U.S. startups. These include established crowdfunding company IndieGogo, however market leader Kickstarter has said that it does not intend to go into equity crowdfunding. There may be requirements or advantages to being a registered broker/ dealer, making it easier for established securities companies to participate in this space.

As we anticipated in the first edition of this book, the U.S. legislative move has encouraged a more open approach to equity crowdfunding in other jurisdictions, with the U.K. Financial Services Authority easing requirements this year, and a revision of New Zealand's securities laws opening the doors to equity crowdfunding, among other recent moves.

The equity crowdfunding landscape will continue to evolve swiftly, with still much uncertainty on the details of the U.S. SEC rulings and how the crowdfunding platform and investment market will subsequently evolve.

> ❝ *I worry about websites popping up all over the place and disappearing and then the money is gone.* ❞
>
> **Meredith Cross**, Director of Corporation Finance,
> U.S. Securities and Exchange Commission

Issues with equity crowdfunding

One of the key challenges for entrepreneurs and business owners is access to capital. Many business owners are unable to obtain funding from traditional investment sources and an estimated 99% of new business ideas go unfunded as a result. As such, obtaining many small investments through crowdfunding is potentially a powerful funding opportunity for many of these businesses.

In most countries, unlisted private companies are unable to sell equity or debt to the public. This means that while companies are able to request money from the public, they are unable to offer shares or bonds in exchange for that funding. If business owners can't offer investors a stake in their businesses, then they are extremely limited in their ability to raise funds.

Laws that prevent crowdfunding exist to maintain fair, orderly, and efficient markets. In the U.S., for example, the Securities and Exchange Commission (SEC) maintains the reporting requirements of public companies, ensuring that public investors are clearly informed about their investments. In addition, stockmarkets such as NYSE and NASDAQ have both minimum market capitalization and revenue requirements for companies to sell shares on their markets, preventing smaller, riskier firms from participating. These regulations increase the burden on companies, but they exist to:

- **Protect the investor**
  By enforcing minimum capitalization and revenue requirements the regulators ensure that only established, and therefore lower-risk, companies can obtain funding from the public

- **Maintain confidence through information**
  Regulators enable investors to make informed investment decisions by ensuring the ongoing flow of standardized information on the performance of companies

- **Manage logistics for the markets**
  The stockmarkets and associated clearing houses manage the transactions and communication with large pools of investors

There are good reasons for regulations around the direct sales of equity to the public. However unlisted companies can sell their shares to one of two groups:

1   Friends, family, or others who have a pre-existing relationship to the business owners;

2   Highly qualified investors who meet either minimum asset holding or minimum income requirements.

Traditional crowdfunding platforms, covered in the previous chapter, are commonly used for funding not-for-profit projects. These cannot be used by companies to raise equity funding from the public. However a number of equity crowdfunding platforms are helping for-profit businesses to obtain equity funding from the crowd by tapping investments from authorized investors.

Current models of crowdfunding

Until true crowdfunding structures emerge, there are three ways in which crowdfunding platforms enable the public sale of debt or equity in privately held companies:

- Selling to a private network

- Selling to highly qualified investors

- Indirect investment in the business

Selling debt or equity to a private network

In many countries, business owners and entrepreneurs can approach an unlimited number of people within their personal network for funding. They can do this as long as the person being offered shares has a pre-existing relationship with the business owner. Some crowdfunding platforms have been launched to manage the process of making investment offers to the business owner's personal network.

Example: 40Billion.com (www.40billion.com)

40Billion.com (named after the estimated $40 billion funding gap for startup entrepreneurs in the U.S.) was launched in July 2008 to allow entrepreneurs to raise money more easily from their friends and family. 40Billion.com provides a set of online tools to create and manage a fund raising within the owners' private networks. The business owners state how much capital they require, select the type of funding they need, list their potential investors, and outline their business plan on the 40Billion.com portal. 40Billion.com then invites the potential funders to join the private investment community and manages the process of building the investment.

To date, 40Billion.com has helped U.S. businesses request $45m in funding from their private networks.

Type of investment	Investors give donations, buy commercial paper (30 to 270 day term), or make direct loans (1 to 3 year term).
Level of total funding available	Up to $1 million (the maximum investment from private networks allowed under U.S. law).
Funding per investor / donor	$25 to $1 million.
Fees	No fees at present, however, this is expected to change as the site becomes more established.
Geographic focus	Businesses who use this service must be U.S.-based.
Similar models	**CapAngel** (France): **www.capangel.com** **Crowdcube** (United Kingdom): **www.crowdcube.com** **ProFounder** (International): **www.profounder.com**

Selling debt or equity to highly qualified investors

Selling debt or equity to qualified investors is also possible in many countries. In the U.S., qualified investors are those with either $1 million in assets or personal annual income of $200,000. Business angel networks already match entrepreneurs with potential investors. In many ways a crowd of highly qualified investors is effectively a virtual business angel network.

Example: SeedUps (www.seedups.com)

SeedUps is a matching engine for entrepreneurs who wish to raise up to £250,000 from high net worth investors. SeedUps was launched in November 2010 and serves British, American, and Irish startups by matching them with potential investors. Entrepreneurs submit a single page opportunity snapshot to the investment portal, which the SeedUps matching engine uses to match entrepreneurs with appropriate investors. SeedUps' all-or-nothing funding model means that the target investment goal must be achieved within 180 days for the investment to go ahead.

To date, over 800 companies have raised over £21 million from over 340 investors through SeedUps.

Type of investment	Equity.
Level of total funding available	Up to £250,000.
Funding per investor / donor	Amounts between £250 and £10,000.
Fees	Free to list a business idea, however successful companies and investors each pay a 2% success fee.
Geographic focus	Businesses based in the U.K., the U.S., and Ireland.
Similar models	**ASSOB** (Australia): **www.assob.com.au** **Innovestment** (Germany): **www.innovestment.de**

Indirect investment in the business

This model of funding involves creating a separate vehicle (an investment company) that invests in the underlying business. The investment vehicle could be a pre-existing fund or a specially created company for the investment opportunity that achieves the highest level of interest from the crowd. In this model the funding will often come from the crowd, in a similar way to a managed fund, however the wisdom of the crowd determines which investments to make.

Example: WiSEED (www.wiseed.fr)

WiSEED is a platform that lists startup businesses looking for funding. WiSEED investors select the companies that interest them and state how much they are willing to invest in each one (upwards of €100). When a business gets the required commitments from investors, WiSEED creates a dedicated investment vehicle with each investor owning a fraction of this investment vehicle. In effect, the investor becomes a shareholder in the investment vehicle that becomes a shareholder in the target company.

To date, 16 startups have achieved a total of €5.1m in investment through WiSEED.

Type of investments	Equity.
Level of total funding available	Upwards of €50,000.
Funding per investor / donor	Upward of €100.
Fees	10% of funding after the fundraising is successful.
Geographic focus	European startups that are younger than 8 years.
Similar companies	**Grow VC** (Global): www.growvc.com **VenCorps** (Global): www.vencorps.com

> 66 *Right now, entrepreneurs like these bakers and these gadget-makers are already using crowdfunding platforms to raise hundreds of thousands of dollars in pure donations – imagine the possibilities if these small-dollar donors became investors with a stake in the venture.*
>
> **White House Office of Science and Technology Report**
> on the American Jobs Act

Where is crowdfunding for businesses going?

At the time of writing, in the U.S. there are a number of proposed changes to the legislation prohibiting crowdfunding, including the White House explicitly linking crowdfunding to President Obama's American Jobs Act, and a Congress bill supporting crowdfunding that is attracting bi-partisan support. As such the U.S. is looking likely to be the first major country to enable equity crowdfunding. Other countries may follow the U.S. lead, however this is likely to take years.

The most likely possible outcomes are:

1 **No regulatory change**

While there appears to be good momentum in the U.S. legislature, there is a good chance that there will be no change to the laws on crowdfunding in most other jurisdictions for the foreseeable future.

2 **Crowd micro-investments allowed**

Equity crowdfunding up to a pre-determined small limit could be allowed, which would minimize downside risk to individual investors. A maximum individual investment of $100 has been mentioned by the White House and other bodies, with suggestions for total investment limits ranging from $100,000 to $1 million.

3 **Larger crowd investments allowed**

Startup Exemption (www.startupexemption.com), an online advocacy group, has petitioned for a limit to individual investments from unaccredited investors of either $10,000 or 10% of their gross income. They have also requested an allowance of up to $5 million in total investments and elimination of the 500 shareholders or less rule for private companies.

Regional variation in crowdfunding regulations

Regulation on crowdfunding regulation varies across developed economies. Below are brief reviews of the situation in some major jurisdictions.

The United States

As discussed earlier in this chapter, the JOBS Act will allow a limited scope of equity crowdfunding in 2013 after the SEC has made specific rulings. In the meantime, the two ways in which U.S. companies can sell debt or equity without having to be a public company and register with the SEC are raising less than $1 million over a 12 month period from people with whom the business has a "substantial, pre-existing relationship", and raising only from "sophisticated" investors.

Europe

The European Union's Prospectus Directive means that any offer of shares or bonds to the public in Europe must be made in a prospectus. Start-ups looking to crowdfund need to draft an expensive prospectus, unless they ask for less than €2.5 million within 12 months in amounts over €50,000. Any request without a prospectus must be directed at less than 100 people in each country in Europe or only made to qualified investors.

Switzerland

Unlike in other European countries, it is possible to raise investment from the crowd in Switzerland provided that any crowdfunding platform does not act as a fund or provide funding directly. Business owners are required to provide a detailed prospectus for all investment.

Australia

Private Australian companies can raise no more than A$2 million over a rolling 12-month period and they must not raise this money from more than 20 people. Australian businesses may raise up to A$5 million from sophisticated, overseas, or professional investors.

> ❝ *The benefits of such a large investor network are that it will bring in new contacts and experience and will build a stronger support ecosystem.* ❞
> **Charles Armstrong**, Founder and Chairman, Trampoline Systems

Factors to consider when crowdfunding

When a business's managers are deciding on the best way to fund its growth, they need to consider not only how to attract funding at the lowest cost, but also the implications of using equity crowdfunding. There are a number of aspects of crowdfunding relative to traditional funding approaches that should be considered.

Challenges of crowdfunding

By its nature, crowdfunding requires company management to communicate with a considerably wider pool of investors. This creates greater complexity in four ways:

1   **The structure of the agreement**

The terms of investments for crowdfunding need to be crafted to ensure that potential investors are clear on their decision-making rights and on the terms of their investment. When working with a small set of investors, it is possible to allow more flexibility in the investment agreement because problems can be resolved with one-on-one discussions.

2   **Communication to large pools of investors**

Companies need to communicate well with their investors. Expectations on the degree and type of communication that crowd investors will receive should be established upfront in the investor agreement. However there are real costs to communicating with investors, and broadening the investor pool without solid communication protocols can greatly increase the burden on the business.

3   **Management of changes to the business**

Investors from the crowd will have invested with expectations of returns, investment timeframe, and in a proposed business strategy. Unlike working with a small set of investors, if the business strategy or the nature of the investment changes, then businesses will have to get approval from many investors or bring in new investors to replace the previous ones.

4   **Secondary markets**

While there are some established secondary markets for equity in private companies, they are not set up for micro-investments in small companies. The lack of a viable secondary market will complicate and inhibit attracting investors.

Benefits of crowdfunding

There are several benefits of crowdfunding compared with other methods of financing. Just as attracting venture capital is perceived to offer advantages to a company, such as access to expertise and networks, crowdfunding offers its own advantages, including:

1   **Testing ideas**

Unlike business angel or venture capital funding, a crowdfunded idea needs a broad base of people who support the idea. As such, crowdfunding brings not only capital, but also confirmation that many people consider the business idea sound. Likewise, a business idea that fails to gain support from the crowd should accept that feedback and refine their business model.

2   **Developing a customer base**

The best source of crowdfunding is from potential customers who see value in the business and what they provide, and have a vested interest in the company succeeding. The crowdfunding process will result in informed and interested investors, and can also assist in generating new customers for its offerings.

3   **Developing a support network**

In the same way that angel investors bring expertise and a network of contacts to a young business, crowdfunding has the potential to give access to a broad network of people who can provide support to the business through advice, services, and promotional activities.

PART VII

USING OTHER PLATFORMS

CROWD BUSINESS MODELS

USING OTHER PLATFORMS

VII

CROWDFUNDING

MANAGING PROJECTS

USING SERVICE MARKETPLACES

BUILDING RELATIONSHIPS

APPLICATIONS OF CROWDSOURCING

FUNDAMENTALS OF CROWDS

Using competition platforms

21

" 99designs is a great place to find designers to work with in the future. Even if that person doesn't win the contest, you can contact them and let them know you like their work. For the designers, it's a great place to create leads for new clients. "

Jack Liu, Chief Community Officer, TeenBusinessForum

Competitions are a powerful method for small businesses to access the skills of creative people in fields such as design and marketing. They can also be a good way to find talented providers for long-term relationships. However running competitions is a participatory sport. You have to be actively engaged throughout the process to get good results.

Chapter overview

- Competition platforms tend to focus on creative projects, such as design, marketing, brand naming, and video production.

- For the best results know what you want beforehand, pick a relevant platform, and prepare to set aside some time.

- You want to attract the best entrants so pay appropriately, write a great design brief, and invite good providers to participate.

- During the contest give feedback consistently as this steers providers to giving you a better result.

- Always pick a winner and get many opinions before making a final selection.

CASE STUDY

How Sarah Sturtevant used a competition to find a designer

Sarah Sturtevant is the founder of Integrated Marketing Solutions Inc, a Canadian-based web marketing consultancy. She was looking for a new company logo so she decided to post a competition on crowdSPRING.

For the first 48 hours she didn't get any responses at all which she found slightly disheartening. Prompted by a suggestion on the crowdSPRING website, she decided to review some of the profiles of providers on the platform and invite them to enter the competition.

Despite getting one very curt refusal from one invitee, the logo designs started to roll in. At the half-way mark she had 29 entries. As she went along she rated each design between 1 and 5, an important indicator to the individuals of which designs she liked. With low scoring entries she also included a few words of feedback, so they could modify entries accordingly.

The vast majority of designs came in the later stages. In the end she had 122 entrants competing for the $375 USD prize.

The winning entry came from a designer based in California who was one of the people who Sturtevant had invited to enter the competition after she had looked at his portfolio. He had an established background, including roles as staff art director for Rolling Stone and at the New York Times.

He had become a stay-at-home dad in his fifties and was producing fine art, but needed commercial work to pay the bills. Winning 37 contests in 8 months on crowdSPRING had helped, but of equal benefit to him had been the ability to connect to new clients through the contests.

Subsequently Sturtevant is talking to the provider about designing her letterhead, business cards, and website banners. She views the whole experience as a very positive one.

Fundamentals of competitions

The principle of competitions is very simply offering a prize for the winning entry to a defined task. This is clearly not a new idea. Early instances of competitions are the Longitude Prize, in which the British government in 1714 offered a £25,000 reward for whoever could provide a reliable way to calculate a vessel's longitude, and French Emperor Louis Napoleon III's 1869 offer of a prize for a butter substitute, which soon resulted in the creation of margarine.

While large-scale competitions such as these are still used, online platforms now enable competitions to be run for a wide variety of small creative tasks. These tap large crowds of providers from which the best work can surface.

How competitions work

Based on information contained in the brief, individuals enter the contest, get feedback from the client, and submit revised entries if they wish. The client then chooses a winner who gets a pre-defined reward. In some cases runners-up are also given prizes, or a broader range or participants are given payment for participating. The client gets the design or new idea and owns the copyright.

There are a number of web platforms that facilitate this process, with some of them focusing on one particular area such as graphic design, video production, or data analytics. The platform has a pre-registered crowd of workers, and also provides the technology that allows the competition to be run effectively.

Some approaches to distributed innovation also use competitions. Chapter 22 on Distributed innovation examines this in more detail. Data analytics competition platform Kaggle is also described in more detail in Chapter 24.

Conceptual overview of competition platforms

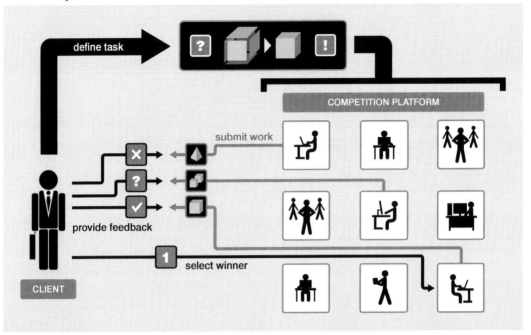

Benefits

Using a competition platform allows especially smaller businesses to be exposed to a wide variety of ideas and approaches that may not be available in-house or from a single provider. They also provide the opportunity to find and build relationships with providers whose style and approach is a good match with the client.

Using a competition platform is usually significantly less expensive than going to a traditional design agency for straightforward tasks such as product logo design. However it is also important to recognize that there can be substantial value created by design agencies, not least in creating a brief that is aligned with the client organization and its strategy. While some design jobs are appropriate for competition platforms on which there is limited scope for interaction with the designers, there are also some jobs that are best done by providers who can use a deep understanding of their client as context for any work done.

For providers, competition platforms provide an opportunity to add to their portfolio, establish relationships, develop skills, and build their reputation. However they are controversial. There are many in the graphic design community who refuse to participate in competitions and actively lobby against them. They believe that participating in competitions devalues the work of professionals because they are providing "on spec" work that they will likely not be paid for, as well as leaving them open to intellectual property theft. See also Chapter 4 for a discussion of some of the ethical controversies surrounding competitions.

Large-scale competitions

While small design and content competitions are proliferating on the new competition platforms, some larger competitions are still being run using traditional approaches where competitors deal directly with the client. However an increasing proportion of corporate competitions are shifting over to the competition platforms, as they can handle all the logistics required, and have an existing pool of people keen to contribute. Companies including Unilever and The Financial Times have used competition platforms for tasks such as designing a concept for a TV advertising campaign.

Types of competitions

Competitions can be used for a wide variety of tasks. The most common application is graphic design, as the format is very well suited to a competition process. There are a wide variety of competition platforms that have been launched in other domains, and no doubt competitions will be applied to many other creative tasks in years to come. Below are some of the existing types of competition with a few representative examples of platforms.

Common competition types

TYPE	DELIVERABLES	EXAMPLE PLATFORMS
Graphic design	Logos, website themes.	99designs DesignCrowd crowdSPRING Guerra Creativa Freelancer.com
Writing	Blog posts, books.	crowdSPRING
Marketing concepts	Brand concepts, advertising campaigns, slogans.	Idea Bounty BootB
Music	Music for commercial use.	Minimum Noise
Video production	Commercials, promotional videos.	Poptent Brandfighters
Names	Product and company names.	Squadhelp Naming Force
IT Projects	Apps, algorithms, analytics, platforms.	TopCoder
Data analytics	Statistics, forecasting, models.	Kaggle

Preparing for a competition

You can maximize your chances of getting a successful outcome by putting in some preparation, rather than launching straight into the competition process. Here are some of the steps worth doing before the competition begins.

Develop a clear idea of what you want

For the best results, try to generate a good idea of what you are looking for prior to the start of the contest. Although that often becomes clearer when you can respond to specific ideas, the more refined your initial ideas, the easier the process becomes. In particular for logo designs, you need to understand and be able to communicate effectively what fits and doesn't fit with the identity of your company or products.

Set aside some time

Using a competition site does require an investment of time. It's usual to get many entries, in some cases well over 100. Considering the merits of each submission as well as giving prompt feedback can be time consuming. This time investment is part of what is required to get good results, so make sure you are not going to be too busy to respond to submissions.

Pick your platform

Competition platforms add value not just by accessing a pool of talented participants, but also by providing a well-structured process of posting projects and viewing competition entries. They differ in their areas of specialization, the number and quality of providers, and some aspects of the competition process and workflow. Look at competitions under way, winning entries, and if you will have several jobs to do, try different platforms to see which works best for you.

Write a detailed brief

The brief you write is all the providers have to go on. Unless you give a good understanding of the context of your competition and what you want from it, you are unlikely to get much that is useful. Most of the competition platforms provide templates that ask detailed questions, for example for a logo design competition who is the target audience, your competition, desired colors, what you do want, what you don't want, and so on. Put in the effort to answer these questions. As well as you can, make the competition and its outcomes sound interesting and engaging.

Posting your contest

Once you have selected a platform and defined what you want, it is time to post your contest on the platform. Here are a few pointers on how to get the best results.

Pay a good price

You should almost always offer more than the average fee on the site. Unless you get good providers attracted to enter the competition, you won't get good results. You don't necessarily have to pay among the highest fees on offer, though if you can afford it the additional investment will draw out the best providers who only participate when the prize is worth going for, and can be well worthwhile. If you can make the project interesting and the competition process engaging, you will still get good designers involved. Browsing previously posted projects will give you an idea of usual fee levels.

Guarantee your budget

Most platforms allow you to guarantee your budget for a competition, so providers know that someone will win the prize. This demonstrates your commitment to the process, makes you more interested yourself in making it successful, and will definitely attract higher quality providers to your project. In any case you should always choose a winner, even if the outcomes weren't quite what you were looking for.

Invite providers to work on your project

Some of the sites have directories of providers you can browse through, so you can invite providers with portfolios that you like. Providers usually respond well to personal invites, as long as the prize on offer is sufficient to interest them.

Don't worry too much about the time

Contests have a default duration, and unless you are in a hurry it is worth sticking with the usual length. For design competitions around seven days is often adequate to get high quality entries. Longer competitions do not usually result in better outcomes. You may also find that the majority of entries (including the best ones) tend to come later in the contest than right at the beginning. Avoid extending the duration if possible, as participants who were expecting a prize to be awarded will quite possibly lose interest.

Focus the competition on one type of task

It's best to focus each competition on one type of task. Providers may specialize in certain kinds of work and you don't want to get output where one part of the deliverable is excellent, and another part less so. Also if you are asking for too broad a task, some providers may not want to enter because of the amount of work involved.

Decide whether the contest is open or closed

Most platforms will allow you to declare whether the contest is open or closed. Open contests allow those entering to see each other's entries and often the feedback others receive. Closed contests keep the entries private. The advantages of an open contest to you is that realistically entrants will look at each other's entries and your advice to them and will use that to refine their own entries. The disadvantage is you may start to get elements of plagiarism in entries, and you are cutting yourself off from those usually talented providers who only enter closed competitions, as they believe others may steal their ideas.

Probably the most important thing that a buyer can do to be successful is to be engaged. Designers can't design in a vacuum. The more feedback and engagement that a buyer can provide in the course of the project, the higher the quality of the designs that will be submitted and the greater the likelihood of success.

Mike Samson, CEO, crowdSPRING

During the contest

During the competition you will be interacting with the crowd. This is perhaps the most important stage of attracting and developing the high quality entries that will meet or exceed your expectations.

Provide detailed feedback

The more feedback you give, the more quality submissions you will get. Creative people don't work well in a void, and good feedback on designs gets a great response. Thank people for their submissions and efforts, and be respectful.

Focus on the good designers

You can usually instantly tell from a submission whether a provider is competent. It is good to give feedback to all initially, even if it is just to point out to all what is wrong with the submission. However from the many entrants competing, you can often clearly see early on who has the capabilities to win.

Give them detailed feedback and specific encouragement to refine their submissions. Remember they have many competitions to choose from, and you want them to be putting energy into yours. Providing feedback and genuine engagement encourages these entrants.

Use the star rating system and withdraw entries

When you have many entries it is difficult to provide individual comments on every entry. If it is an open content then providing some more detailed feedback earlier on gives all the entrants more clues to what you want. Later on, it is more important simply to indicate what you like and don't like.

Some sites have rating systems. It takes a moment to give a star rating and give very useful feedback to entrants. If it's clear that particular providers will never get there, just withdraw them. That provides clear feedback for everybody.

Get multiple opinions as you consider submissions

It can get overwhelming once you've looked at over 100 entries, and it's important to get multiple perspectives on what's on offer. Get opinions and suggestions from your team, friends and customers. What is being created will be seen by many people, so you want many opinions. Most platforms allow you to share selected submissions with your community so they can vote on their most popular ones.

Picking the winner

So prepare the drum roll, open the golden envelope, it's time to announce the winner! But sometimes it's not as straightforward as it might seem. You might be struggling to work out just who should win, some entries may seem strangely familiar, or you may feel underwhelmed at the quality of entries.

Always select a winner

Competition platforms often allow you not to select a winner if you haven't guaranteed the prize, but don't do it. You should pay for the best design. It's not fair on the designers if you don't select a winner, and you are not likely to get decent submissions if you use the service again later. If you have already guaranteed that you will pay then this is not an issue.

Compensate those that contributed

In an open contest it may be that some entries have built on others. If this is the case you should give a prize to those whose creative input clearly influenced the winning design. You may also choose to give prizes to the runners up. Most platforms allow you to allocate prizes, and in some cases build in rewards to more than just the individual winner.

Consider getting the winner to work on it more

If you have a clear winner from the competition, you might still want to try a few variations on the ideas or to develop it a little further. Offer to pay the winner a small amount extra to work through some other possibilities, to make sure you have the best version of the design.

Use competition platforms to find providers for other work

Competition platforms can be great for defined high-visibility projects, particularly in design areas such as logos, business cards, or flyers. But for many tasks it is easier to work with a single designer, particularly once they get to know you well.

One of the best reasons to use a competition platform is to find great designers you can work with on other projects. You can invite them to work for you directly or through an established service marketplace. Some of the competition platforms are establishing platforms to build an ongoing relationship with providers after you have discovered their talent in a competition.

Check for plagiarism

You can expose yourself if you don't check the winner for plagiarism. Unfortunately it does happen. If it is a design competition, tools such as reverse image search on Google or TinEye allow you to find whether the image has already appeared on the web, and a variety of plagiarism detectors can uncover whether text is original.

Using distributed innovation

22

> " Open innovation argues that the future belongs to those who do the best job of integrating the best of their internal ideas and capabilities with the best external ideas and capabilities. Designing and orchestrating a global network of capabilities is the basis for a brighter future for us all. "
>
> **Henry Chesbrough,** Executive Director, Center for Open Innovation at the Haas School of Business, University of California

The ability to innovate is becoming perhaps the most important driver of organizational success. Crowdsourcing mechanisms provide an excellent opportunity to tap internal and external insights to solve problems, create or enhance products, and make better decisions. Distributed innovation is an increasingly important dimension to how organizations can draw on the power of crowds.

Chapter overview

- The imperative of innovation in today's economy means distributed innovation processes that access the best ideas inside and outside the organization are increasingly vital to success.

- Innovation markets are often used by larger organizations to post research challenges aimed at academic, technical, and other specialist teams.

- Idea management platforms facilitate the ongoing submission of ideas from targeted communities that propose and rank the best ideas.

- Prediction markets allow crowds to predict the likelihood of events, with a wide variety of applications such as sales forecasting.

CASE
STUDY

How NASA used distributed innovation to solve a thirty year-old problem

Levels of solar activity impact many things, including weather and climate. With manned and unmanned exploration of the solar system, high solar activity could expose astronauts to severe radiation and increase the risk of technology malfunctioning.

For thirty years NASA has grappled with the issue of how accurately to predict solar activity in very short time frames to determine the optimum time for launching spacecraft and conducting missions. This was one of the challenges that NASA decided to post on the distributed innovation platform InnoCentive.

NASA has been an active supporter of using distributed innovation and competitions to solve specific issues it is facing. For example in the past six years it has set a number of "Centennial Challenges" based around different themes, including "Sample Return Robot" and "Nano-Satellite Launch".

They have also set up their own branded 'pavilion' within InnoCentive that displays their current areas of interest. These have ranged from new packing technologies that keep food in space fresher for longer to the "co-ordination of sensor swarms for extra-terrestrial research." In the pavilion they also posted their request for "Data driven forecasting of solar events."

The winner of the challenge was Bruce Cragin, a retired radio frequency engineer from New Hampshire, US. He was awarded a $30,000 prize for being able to predict the "onset, intensity of duration" of a "solar event" with 75% accuracy within a 24 hour forecast window.

What makes the challenge so remarkable is that a solution has eluded NASA's own scientists for so long.

Aneesh Chopra, the Federal Chief Technology Officer of the United States, commented that all the engineer needed "was a simple Internet connection. No complicated RFP, the need for a lobbyist, some convoluted process – just a smart person in our country who could help solve a difficult scientific challenge and was paid a modest $30,000 for that insight."

> **❝** *No matter who you are, most of the smartest people work for someone else.* **❞**
> **Bill Joy**, Co-Founder, Sun Microsystems

Fundamentals of distributed innovation

Innovation will be fundamental to every organization's success in the 21st century. Globalization, free information flow, increased competition, and heightened expectations from customers mean that organizations that do not consistently innovate will struggle to succeed or even to survive. In a connected world, innovation requires both increasing specialization, and accessing the talents of the broadest possible pool of experts.

The employees of large or even medium-sized organizations can be viewed as crowds that can be tapped for their collective insight. Perhaps more importantly, the concept of open innovation suggests that companies need to look outside their organizations for the expertise and creativity that will drive their business forward.

Principles for value creation

The broader idea of distributed innovation encompasses drawing on both internal and external crowds to generate valuable new ideas, products, processes, strategies, and other outcomes that are critical for success. Below are some of the core principles for creating value from distributed innovation.

Tap a wide and diverse audience

In most cases distributed innovation should tap as wide and diverse an audience as possible. While some areas of innovation are extremely specialized, in many cases the most valuable and useful ideas come from people who work outside that domain who can bring new perspectives to bear. Consider including people from distinctly different areas of expertise in the pool you draw on as they may have highly original and relevant insights.

Internal and external

Insights can come from both inside and outside an organization. Depending on the type of innovation you are looking to generate, you should select which of these is the immediate priority, or decide to go immediately to both.

Employees are an excellent source of creative thinking. The creative potential within the staff of almost all organizations is barely tapped, and there are many approaches to draw out useful innovation from current employees. Challenge-based competitions, innovation programs, idea management platforms, and prediction markets have been widely used in many organizations and often yield valuable results. The outcome of the process is not just the value of the ideas generated, but also building greater engagement with staff who are able to exercise their creativity and imagination and feel that they are valued and contributing significantly to the organization.

Smaller companies and organizations that have very specific challenges will usually have to go outside to get access to the quantity and diversity of ideas that may generate results.

Different models

There are three major models for distributed innovation platforms, although they have some similarities and overlap.

- **Innovation markets**

  Sometimes referred to as R&D platforms, these are essentially competition platforms that are focused on specific challenges posted by an organization. Usually a pre-specified reward is given to whoever meets the challenge or provides the best idea. They are commonly used by larger organizations for high-value R&D activities, such as new product development processes that require technical or academic expertise.

- **Idea management**

  Moving on from the suggestion box, many organizations now use platforms that allow internal or external communities to contribute ideas, which are then debated, developed, and voted on. Idea management platforms are commonly used to source suggestions from employees, as well as to engage with customer communities.

- **Prediction markets**

  Internal or external crowds can collectively predict the outcome of specified events, usually through a market-based mechanism of buying and selling the likelihood of that event happening.

Market maturity

Some aspects of distributed innovation are relatively mature. Idea management platforms such as Imaginatik have been around for 15 years, while InnoCentive publicly launched in 2001. Prediction markets have been used in the corporate arena for over two decades, though it is only over the last five years or so that a range of commercial prediction market platforms have become available.

Innovation markets

Innovation markets are typically used by larger organizations to support their research and development operations, though are also increasingly used by smaller companies as an accessible approach to innovation. There are a number of public innovation markets on which organizations can post their challenges. Some companies such as Procter & Gamble have created their own corporate-branded sites.

Typical challenges include:

- Scientific and technical problems
- New product development
- Marketing, branding, and process improvement solutions
- Broader social and environmental issues

Process

The underlying process of distributed innovation platforms is in essence the same as competition platforms, however there are a few significant distinctions.

Innovation markets: Process overview	
Registered crowd	Large numbers of individuals are registered to provide ideas or solutions for challenges. Depending on the type of platform these participants may be highly specialized in technical or academic fields.
Post challenge	An organization posts a highly defined challenge, usually with a pre-defined reward for the best idea or one that meets the challenge.
Search and connect	Individuals and teams search through and identify challenges that are relevant or interesting to them. Some innovation markets encourage individuals and teams to connect with each other and collaborate to develop responses to the challenges.
Submit ideas	The participants submit ideas or solutions based on the challenge.
Review and interact	The ideas are reviewed by the seekers. During this period there may be some interaction with the seekers to give feedback, clarify points, or develop ideas, usually within a facilitated online workspace.
Reward	The seekers select a winner or verify that the solution meets the specified challenge. The winner is paid the specified reward for the best submission or solution.
Transfer IP	In general, full intellectual property rights for the winning solution become the property of the client organization. Those who did not win retain the rights to their ideas or proposed solutions.

Posting your challenge

Since innovation markets in most cases have essentially the same structure as competition platforms, much of the advice given in Chapter 21 also applies here. Here we review the most important issues and look at how some of these apply in the distinct case of innovation markets.

Be precise

Precision is fundamental for innovation markets. For technical challenges in particular, you should be able to express the challenge in such a way that it is completely unambiguous whether an entry meets the criteria to win the prize. In particular any constraints, such as type of equipment or materials used, must be specified. If there is not a defined threshold to winning the prize and the best solution is sought, then the decision criteria must be as objective as possible.

Protect intellectual property

Particularly in the R&D area, there may be a need to reveal concepts and ideas that are commercially sensitive or partly reveal your own organization's IP or product development pipeline. Often for teams to be able to respond effectively to a challenge they will need access to significant detail.

Most of the innovation markets cover the protection of IP within their process so that the necessary agreements can be approved and steps taken before innovators can access any sensitive content.

Offer attractive rewards

In many cases, particularly in R&D challenges, the motivation of the crowd is primarily financial. The reward should be commensurate with the value of the idea. The best minds and teams are selective about the challenges they will undertake, and as researchers are aware of the value of intellectual property. They will be usually reluctant to undertake research and forgo any IP ownership from that unless there is a compelling reward relative to the effort expended.

Tap intrinsic motivation

There are also opportunities to tap non-financial motivations for solving challenges. Some of the most powerful motivators include contributing to people's health or quality of life, getting explicit recognition for contributions, forming new relationships, and gaining an enhanced reputation among peers or beyond. Consider how you can build these outcomes into the rewards or contribution process.

Examples of innovation markets

Innovation markets generally allow clients and contributors to post and view challenges, give access to a pre-registered crowd of relevant experts, and provide a platform to facilitate collaboration between seekers and solvers. Here is summary information on four prominent innovation markets.

InnoCentive

Formed in 2001 and the current market leader, InnoCentive tends to present technical R&D or scientific challenges from blue chip organizations such as NASA (occasionally in branded 'pavilions'), with bounties which range from $10,000 to $1,000,000. There is a tightly controlled process to protect IP.

ideaken

ideaken is a Software-as-a-Service platform based around collaborative innovation. It is aimed at the enterprise market, but is also used by some smaller organizations. It claims to be both scalable and flexible, allowing for a range of innovation scenarios that can include posting challenges to a nominated set of individuals, internal groups, external communities, or combinations of all these.

NineSigma

NineSigma mainly services large global corporates, for example GlaxoSmithKline, in addition providing a number of value-add services such as consulting, training, and implementation. NineSigma gives access to a network of commercial and academic experts from over 135 different countries. Although the specialists cover diverse sectors and capabilities, NineSigma currently specializes in sustainability issues.

Innovation Exchange

Innovation Exchange describes its client base as "Global 5000 companies and not-for-profit organizations". Financial rewards are usually between $50,000 to $100,000. Challenges cover new product concepts, marketing, and wider social issues such as child poverty. The platform also facilitates social networking, encouraging individual innovators to connect and form teams to respond to challenges.

Idea management

Idea Management (sometimes "ideation") is used to describe the process, systems, and supporting software to generate, assess, filter, and take action on ideas. The platforms were originally primarily used to support idea generation from internal staff. However these platforms, and now some others designed explicitly for the purpose, are often being used to enable external groups such as customers or the general public to contribute ideas.

Process

There are some similarities between idea management and innovation markets, however the emphasis in idea management is far more on collaboration in filtering and developing ideas. In addition financial incentives are usually far less important, or sometimes non-existent. One of the benefits of idea management processes is that they drive engagement from participants and can enable useful connections between innovators.

Idea management: Process overview	
Brand site	The idea management site is usually branded by the sponsoring organization or project.
Define community	A particular community of users will be targeted (e.g. employees, customers, or experts). Some may already be registered on the system, or they may need to be attracted to register.
Provide guidance	The sponsoring organization will describe the scope and intent of the ideas they want to receive.
Submit ideas	Ideas are submitted by individuals.
Community voting and feedback	The community comments on the proposals and votes on the ones they find most relevant.
Idea development	Ideas submitted can be developed or built on by others using a variety of tools including discussions and further idea ranking.
Organization feedback	The sponsoring organization can give feedback on ideas where relevant.
Selection	Taking into account the most popular ideas, the organization selects ideas to take forward and put into action. Progress on which ideas are being implemented and the results are displayed on the site.
Reward and recognition	The originators of successful ideas and other highly active contributors are formally recognized through online points systems, badges, financial prizes, or other rewards.
Analysis	Relevant statistics and performance indicators can be extracted to identify other useful actions and improve the success of subsequent projects.

> *The world is becoming too fast, too complex and too networked for any company to have all the answers inside.*
>
> **Yochai Benkler**, Berkman Professor of Entrepreneurial Legal Studies,
> Harvard University

Customer ideas

Like social media channels, requesting ideas from customers and the public through a structured platform can be a powerful way of creating dialogue and loyalty, as well as a great way to generate innovative ideas. Many companies operate some kind of informal customer suggestion box scheme, but what is done with these ideas is often not highly visible.

Some corporations, such as Cisco with its I-Prize, have attracted significant attention by running ad-hoc contests with attractive financial rewards. Other companies have established platforms for ongoing public idea submission. Two of the best known examples are My Starbucks Idea and Dell's IdeaStorm.

On these platforms members of the public submit ideas, usually about possible new products or features, which are then voted on by the crowd. The submissions are displayed in order of popularity, with comments from the company on how they are responding to the submitted ideas.

These sites work best where there is a passionate and brand-loyal customer community. It is also important that there are clear examples of ideas originating from the public being taken up by the company. Customer idea submission platforms will be counter-productive unless there is clear and tangible evidence that contributions are resulting in real action.

Example: Best Buy Idea X

Best Buy Idea X is consumer products retailer Best Buy's internally built idea management forum for Best Buy customers to post, debate, and vote on ideas about how to improve the consumer experience. Idea submissions are solicited in areas including ways to lower Best Buy's impact on the environment, new products, and suggestions for locations of new stores. Best Buy then offer their feedback.

Within three months of the platform's launch in June 2009, 1,000 ideas had already been submitted. In the first year this had reached over 7,000 with over 2,000 active users. Successful ideas which the platform has helped bring to fruition are a pilot to establish free WiFi in stores, trialling electronic receipts, and a packaging improvement that stemmed from an idea originally submitted as "get rid of those stupid plastic boxes."

Approaches for success

Idea management platforms have many of the same attributes as online community sites and need to be actively managed. Crowds that submit ideas are likely to be loyal to your organization or brand in some way, perhaps as customers or employees, and will expect a reasonable level of communication and engagement.

Idea management: Approaches for success	
Indicate needs	Give indications of the types of ideas that are needed, if useful organizing these into general categories such as 'New Product Ideas'.
Maintain communication	Ensure you are actively communicating with participants, giving reactions and feedback to ideas, and helping to develop these where necessary. This activity needs to be continuous for the site to be perceived as active.
Be open and honest	Some ideas may be critical of the way things are currently being done. Make sure your responses are open and honest, as authentic dialogue is important to the credibility of idea management platforms.
Identify community managers	Improve the experience for the crowd by ensuring that any responses are given by a named individual, who can be recognized as having a community manager role.
Prove ideas make a difference	Demonstrate that ideas are being put into action to keep the crowd engaged. Make sure that examples are visible of contributed ideas that have been implemented.
Create visible online recognition	Recognition is important to the crowd so ensure there are ways to showcase those who have submitted the most popular ideas, as well as the most active contributors. Many platforms have points or badges that can be allocated to successful individuals, with accompanying leaderboards.
Offer non-financial incentives	Where a crowd is loyal to your brand or organization be wary of offering financial incentives, as this can fundamentally alter the dynamic of the platform, often actually discouraging idea submission. Modest prizes and gifts can work.
Vary voting mechanisms	Some platforms have interesting ways to facilitate the voting and rating of ideas, for example using virtual currency. This can keep the crowd engaged, though be careful of making too many changes that could confuse participants.

Examples of idea management platforms

Idea management platforms generally include a site where a relevant community can register, submit ideas, and then discuss, vote, and give feedback on those ideas. Below is summary information on four prominent idea management platforms.

IdeaScale

IdeaScale is a cloud-based solution used by companies to interact with customer communities who are commenting on product developments. It has also been used as a forum for U.S. government initiatives. Features include leaderboards for the most active contributors and a Facebook app. IdeaScale claim they are fully scalable across differing organizational sizes and also offer a freemium model.

Imaginatik

Imaginatik markets itself as "Innovation as a Service", with its platform designed around the typical life cycle of an innovation program. Mainly intended for internal use in larger enterprises, the company also provides a range of consulting services. Imaginatik has been providing idea management platforms for over 15 years.

Spigit

Founded in 2007, Spigit's platform is aimed at larger enterprises. It has a series of branded products that can be applied to a range of scenarios, both internally and externally-focused. Features include an algorithm called RepUrank which assesses employee's contributions and allocates them a score. Participants can also use a variety of voting techniques to show support for ideas, for example by using a virtual currency to trade ideas and allocate budgets to projects.

Qmarkets

Qmarkets bills itself as providing "collective wisdom solutions". In addition to standard idea management functionality it also includes a prediction market platform. It offers incentive programs and the ability to view individuals' forecasting success.

Prediction markets

Prediction markets are platforms that aggregate diverse opinions to predict outcomes or the likelihood of events. They usually are based on a market structure in which participants 'invest' based on their view on how likely it is that a defined outcome will occur. This structure effectively brings together many participants' opinions, in exactly the same way that the prices in a futures market express aggregate views on future prices.

Internet-based prediction markets have been around for close to two decades, initially being used to predict domains such as political elections (Iowa Electronic Market) and the success of movies (Hollywood Stock Exchange). Over the last decade a wide variety of platforms have become available, facilitating the internal and external use of prediction markets by companies. There are a wide range of corporate applications for prediction markets.

For example, technology companies Oracle and Hewlett-Packard have used prediction markets to forecast sales figures. Sales for coming quarters are notoriously difficult to forecast accurately, as any aggregation of individual or team's targeted sales figures will reflect built-in incentives for mis-reporting. However if individuals are asked to predict the sales figures for a division or the company as a whole, they are collectively likely to have sufficient information to make very accurate forecasts.

Other internal applications for prediction markets have included General Electric generating new business ideas, Starwood selecting marketing campaigns, and Google forecasting actual product launch dates compared to scheduled ones.

Prediction market platforms

Companies that provide prediction market platforms include Consensus Point, Crowdcast, Inkling Markets, Intrade, NewsFutures, and Xpree. As noted earlier in this chapter, some idea management platforms such as Qmarkets incorporate prediction markets, partly as a way to predict which ideas are most likely to actually get through to the market and be successful.

Using microtask platforms

23

> *Yesterday I tried using Amazon's Mechanical Turk service for the first time to save myself from some data collection drudgery. I found it fascinating. For the right kind of task, and with a little bit of setup effort, it can drastically reduce the cost and hassle of getting good data compared to other methods.*
>
> **Andy Eggers**, Lecturer, London School of Economics

Microtask platforms take projects and reduce them to a series of small, well-defined tasks that are distributed to workers all over the globe. The ability to allocate microtasks to many workers is likely to have a major impact, as business processes are increasingly broken into small pieces that are allocated as appropriate to computers or humans, and distributed around the world.

Chapter overview

- Microtask platforms are suited for a range of tasks including data gathering and checking, content management, and search engine optimization tasks.

- The first-launched and largest microtask platform is Amazon Mechanical Turk, however there are now a number of other platforms available.

- Tasks need to be as objective as possible for the best results.

- Data quality is a major issue, requiring effective strategies for quality checking when using microtask platforms.

- The APIs on microtask platforms can be used to significantly improve the efficiency and performance of many business processes.

- Using value-add aggregators to manage microtask platforms and providers can minimize effort and risk in creating value from microtasks.

CASE
STUDY

How Shiny Orb used Mechanical Amazon Turk to improve their website:

"On our website www.ShinyOrb.com, we have an attribute-based search, where brides and bridesmaids can find wedding apparel based on dress criteria, such as length or neckline. This requires us to tag every dress with a length, a neckline, and a sleeve type. We decided to try Mechanical Turk to categorize our dresses.

We quickly found that the biggest problem with this crowdsourcing concept is monitoring quality. How could we make sure that each worker catego-rized the length, neckline, and sleeves correctly? We did a few experiments to try to improve quality. We've found that price makes no difference when you're talking about super cheap, super fast gigs.

For Shiny Orb, we ran two price tests. We first paid $0.03 to get the length, neckline, and sleeves classifications for each dress. For the second test, we decided to offer $0.01 for all three. We found no difference in quality, The downside to offering less compensation is that fewer workers do your gigs, making it slower to receive results. Still, we had no problem getting all dresses categorized within half a day.

From our tests, clarity affects quality more than anything else. By that I mean, we found significant improvement in results by clarifying the definitions for our categories and placing those definitions upfront and center.

In particular, in our first Turk test, one of the choices we had for neckline and sleeves was "Other," which workers tended to select a lot. Our success rate of correct categorizations for that test was:
- *92% for length, 64% for neckline, and 64% for sleeves*

In our second test, we made it very clear that "Other" basically shouldn't be chosen, which increased our success rate in the neckline and sleeves categories to:
- 90% for length, 86% for neckline, and 87% for sleeves

Lastly, we found that in order to get these fairly high quality numbers, we had to run the same gig with three workers. I.e. have three workers categorize each dress. We took the majority "vote" of the categories and found this to improve our quality significantly."

Jennifer Chin and **Elizabeth Yin**, Founders, LaunchBit.com

Fundamentals of microtask platforms

Microtask platforms are generally used for small, well-defined, repetitive tasks that usually do not require significant skills. These are applied within ongoing business processes or in some cases as part of a single project.

The basic model is that large projects are broken down into small constituent tasks, called microtasks, which are distributed to a large crowd of registered workers who work on them simultaneously.

Creating value with microtask platforms	
Reduced cost	Costs savings can be significant, with figures often quoted of 50% - 90% savings compared to running the same process in-house or via traditional outsourcing.
Turnaround	As a large labor pool works on tasks simultaneously the turnaround on projects can be very fast, especially if the pool is global and working around the clock.
Process Improvement	Significant improvements in business process performance can be achieved, especially if processes are redesigned to use crowdsourcing effectively, and APIs are used to integrate external work into existing processes.
Data quality	If a project involves data validation, aggregating multiple responses from a large number of people can be more accurate than other methods, such as sampling by highly trained data checkers.
Repeating the process	Establishing microtask projects can be complex, including defining tasks, managing the process, and ensuring data quality. The greatest value comes from frequently repeated or ongoing processes.

Applications of microtasks

There are a wide variety of tasks and functions that can be performed using microtask platforms. The more common ones include data acquisition, data checking, and tasks related to search engine optimization.

The more the project can be broken down into simple microtasks and the higher the number of microtasks, the greater the value that can be created by using microtask platforms. Below are examples of some of the tasks that are well suited to microtask platforms. However there is plenty of scope for imagination in identifying small, well-defined tasks that could be done usefully as a microtask.

Typical microtasks

Content management	▪ Check links. ▪ Check for inappropriate language.
Database creation	▪ Compile lists of companies. ▪ Find phone numbers.
Data management	▪ Add tags and metadata to information. ▪ Verify data and information. ▪ Categorize information. ▪ Check photographs are well framed. ▪ Identify duplicate data.
Text creation	▪ Create catalog descriptions. ▪ Transcription of conversations.
Translation	▪ Translate words. ▪ Translate phrases.
Search engine optimisation	▪ Add tags to content. ▪ Test changes in search results from content changes.
Testing	▪ Test usability of website. ▪ Identify user preferences.

Setting up projects

A major challenge in using microtask platforms is setting up the project and defining the tasks well. Many users report that they get better at it as they gain more experience. One of the key factors is in creating unambiguous instructions that the microtask workers can easily comprehend, as well as framing projects so they will attract and sustain the workers' attention.

Choosing a platform

While there are a fairly small number of dedicated microtask platforms, there are other approaches that can be used to get these kinds of tasks done, as well as aggregators and value-add services that provide interfaces and management to microtask workers.

Microtask platform options

Amazon Mechanical Turk	Mechanical Turk dominates the microtask landscape. It is the longest established platform, draws on a huge labor pool, and has advanced APIs. It describes microtasks as "Human Intelligence Tasks" (HITs). The platform can only be used by project owners with a US-based bank account.
Other microtask platforms	For non- U.S. based project owners and those looking to tap other worker pools there are a variety of other platforms including Clickworker, Microtask, ShortTask, and Samasource.
Service marketplaces	Some employers choose to post what are effectively microtask projects on to the larger service marketplaces, but here you will need to individually manage providers or teams.
Niche platforms	Some niche platforms such as Jana (for researching consumer insights) cover specific types of microtask work.
Aggregators and managed services	Aggregators provide a managed service and platform usually as a layer on top of Amazon Mechanical Turk. These are discussed at the end of this chapter.

Defining microtasks

One of the critical success factors in using microtask platforms is defining the tasks. There is a logical process to follow which breaks down an overall project into small constituent parts, each of which can be posted as tasks. The platforms do have some tools to help you with this, for example Mechanical Turk has a template to follow, however the best starting point is to study tasks other users are posting.

For instance an overall project might be the creation of a database of company data for marketing purposes. Each microtask might be the collation of a piece of data such as the office telephone number, which populates one field of one record in the entire database. If you have 1,000 records, and each record has 10 fields to fill, then you potentially have up to 10,000 microtasks.

There are a number of principles to defining microtasks that will assist in achieving the best outcomes.

Objective tasks

The more objective you can make the task, the more efficient the project will be. For example if you want somebody to rate the usability of a website out of ten, you need to specify exactly what the criteria for the rating are. It is even better to ask the workers to provide some raw information about each page, such as how long it took to navigate from the front page to a specific back page, from which you can then calculate your own rating once the data is returned.

Comparability

Tasks need to be designed so their outputs are directly comparable, and are not dependent on the individual worker. Being able to compare results is fundamental to accurately assessing quality and leveraging the task being performed multiple times.

Use multiple opinions

If some tasks have subjective components, getting multiple responses and doing statistical analysis on average scores and their variation can produce the most useful insights. If this is done on an appropriate scale this can work extremely well. In this case gathering relevant profile information can be useful in determining whether there are meaningful differences. Depending on the task, profile data might include information such as age, technology experience, or even gender.

Time and cost

Microtask definitions need to include a deadline and the expected time a task should take to perform, along with the price paid. Some workers will prefer a high volume of very quick low-cost tasks, whereas others may prefer a smaller number of higher-paying tasks. Of course tasks need to be priced to attract the right calibre of workers.

Label your task

Task descriptors need to be correct to ensure workers who have experience in the work you need will see the job when it is posted, and will be interested in bidding on it.

Monitoring quality

There are very low barriers to entry for microtask workers, so quality is a significant challenge for microtask users. As such project design needs to address quality from the outset and in the entire structure of how work is performed and applied. It is likely you will need to nominate a person to oversee quality assurance for the project. This topic is addressed in more detail in Chapter 18 on Structures and roles.

There are variety of approaches for maintaining quality assurance, however the single most important factor is framing the tasks so that there are objective, comparable, assessable outputs.

Hiring quality checkers

You can hire people on a microtask platform itself to do quality control work and grade the quality of the responses, usually through sampling a certain percentage of a person's work. For very large projects it is also possible to have an extra tier of workers who grade the graders.

Pre-test a subset of your tasks

Quality issues can stem from the task definition. For large projects it is worth testing a smaller sample of the tasks out for real on your microtask platform, and use this as a guide to potentially refine the task itself or change your quality assurance strategy.

It can be worth getting the tasks performed by people you know prior to the exercise. The output or accuracy rates on this sample will give you a reference point for what is submitted by the workers, establishing confidence or indicating that alternative approaches need to be taken.

Redundancy

The cost of microtasks and the intrinsic quality issues mean that one of the most fundamental strategies for microtask work is redundancy: getting more than one worker to carry out the same task. Some clients do this with three workers and then take the majority vote – two out of three – others choose to do it with five or more. The higher the number of people you hire to do the same task, and the higher the level of consensus that you accept as the "correct" answer, the better quality results you will get.

While bringing statistical approaches to bear helps, it is hard to anticipate the realities of microtask process work, so testing a number of tasks and redundancy strategies prior to doing a very large project will help determine the best approach. There can be a drawback to this method on Amazon Mechanical Turk if you have set it up to automatically reject tasks where there isn't a consensus. Workers don't like it because they are open to having their (perfectly good) responses rejected and will not want to work on your project.

Use the gold standard

You may also need strategies to rate the quality of individual workers. A common approach is to use a "Gold Standard", which involves inserting a piece of data into the task for which you know the correct answer. By comparing individuals' responses with the standard answers you can assess their capabilities at this task. This method is not possible for all types of projects, but is in many cases a useful filter.

Predict likeliest answer

Another method is to calculate accuracy based on comparing workers' responses with the most likely answer for parts of a task. The most "likely" answer might be your own estimate or the majority answer provided by the workers. If some workers tend to have a lower rate of predicting the most likely answer, there are implications for quality. Crowdsourcing expert Panos Ipeirotis suggests combining this approach with the "Gold Standard" for the best results.

Sample tasks
All of the above can be time-consuming, and for very large projects more sophisticated quality control methods may best be used on a limited sample of tasks, or restricted to certain parts of a task.

Use the experience of the crowd
You can ask for input from the crowd into various aspects of the project as you go. Collectively they have huge experience, are often motivated by the interaction, and many will give you useful opinions on how best to define a task or other issues. You may choose to build up a pool of trusted workers who you ask for comment on tasks or projects before they commence.

Improving processes
Microtask platforms can be used to improve business processes by making them more efficient, timely, or effective. There are many potential benefits, including taking burden off internal resources, improving outcomes for your customers, and enabling greater flexibility in how processes are performed.

Use microtasks for new activities
For growing businesses using a microtask platform gives access to back-end processes that normally would not be possible due to cost or logistics. Because microtask work is suited to projects relating to data validation and interacting with web pages, there are significant opportunities for sourcing marketing data for focused campaigns, or introducing new web-based services.

Crowdsourcing can be a great enabler, providing the logistical backbone for creating highly innovative approaches in your field. For example CardMunch, now owned by LinkedIn, is an iPhone app which scans business cards and turns them into contact data to add to your systems. The cards are scanned, the images sent to Amazon Mechanical Turk who transcribe the details, and then returned to the user.

Automate processes via an API
To achieve real process improvement and embed microtask platform in your processes you will need to automate your interaction. You can hire experienced developers to use the APIs of the major microtask platforms to build an interface between your systems and the platform.

For example photo-sharing website Snap Mylife used Amazon Mechanical Turk to moderate all their photos. They automated this service using the platform's API, so that when a photo was uploaded it was immediately posted for moderation as a microtask. This not only saved costs, eased the internal burden, and established 24 hour coverage, but also reduced the turnaround time for picture upload to around three minutes. They used lessons from the first phase to further improve the service, again using the API.

Re-engineer your own processes

If parts of your business model rely on crowdsourcing it may be time to look at the way you do things internally. You may need to re-align your own internal processes so they have an optimum fit with the tasks you are getting done externally. This may involve creating new roles or new ways of using the data that emerges from your crowdsourcing initiatives.

Using a crowd process provider

If assessing data quality on a microtask platform sounds daunting, it is worth considering using a 'crowd process' provider, which includes both aggregating microtask platforms as well as performing a range of value-add functions. Some companies will project manage all aspects of a microtask-based assignment from task definition to assessing data quality through to providing the technology platform. Particularly for more complex tasks, the chances of successful outcomes are greatly enhanced by using these services.

When to consider using an aggregator	
One-off project	If you are unlikely to use a microtask platform again.
No in-house resource or skills	No resources for quality control or project management roles.
Fast turnaround	When short deadlines means adequate preparation is not possible.
Disaster recovery	If a project has gone wrong and you need to start again.
Complex project	If you need to target specialist microtask workers.
When you need guarantees	If you need guarantees for levels of data accuracy.

Choose platform

Crowd process providers include CrowdFlower, Data Discoverers, and Scalable Workforce. To a lesser extent some microtask platforms such as Clickworkers or Microtask provide managed services themselves, which cross-over with those provided by the crowd process firms. Each of these companies has particular specialty service types that they promote on their website and through their direct salesforces.

How crowd process providers add value

Crowd process firms effectively take the advantages of leveraging the power of the crowd – such as large throughput and lower cost – and combine these with the convenience and guaranteed service levels of a Business Process Outsourcer.

They principally add value in the areas where experience helps in project design and execution. These include:

- General project management

- Managing data quality

- Defining the microtasks

- Targeting particular types of workers

They also add value structurally through:

- Access to a quality workforce

- Data on the quality of individual workers

- Technology platforms

- Reporting

Use an improved interface

Some of the crowd service firms also provide branded technology platforms, usually as a layer which sits on top of Amazon Mechanical Turk. These can usually be used in a self-service capacity by their clients.

Some of these tend to be aimed at more experienced users, allowing them to track the performance of workers, target the high-performing ones, use communication tools like live chat, and provide a dashboard for both project management and analyzing results.

Aggregators like CrowdFlower also provide a self-service tool to post microtasks, allowing users easily to insert "Gold Standard" data to help assess worker quality.

Other ways crowds create value

24

> *The old-fashioned notion of an individual with a dream of perfection is being replaced by distributed problem solving and team-based multi-disciplinary practice. The reality for advanced design today is dominated by three ideas: distributed, plural, collaborative. It is no longer about one designer, one client, one solution, one place.*
>
> **Bruce Mau**, Founder,
> Institute without Boundaries and Massive Change Network

The concept of crowdsourcing can be applied in many ways. Some approaches to crowdsourcing, such as service marketplaces, competition platforms, and crowdfunding are well established with many alternatives on offer. However there are a wide variety of other ways in which crowds are creating value, just a few of which we describe in this chapter.

Chapter overview

- Over the last few years human imagination and ingenuity have been put to work to identify a plethora of approaches to creating value from crowds.

- Managed crowds can be applied to issues such as testing, consumer research, search engine marketing, and data modelling.

- Translation is one of the domains in which crowdsourcing is being applied, both by companies tapping the energy of their customers as well as through platforms.

- Structures for crowdsourced product design enable those who originate and build on ideas to profit from their contributions.

Can book writing be crowdsourced?

Writing a book is usually the preserve of individuals or very small teams. Other than anthologies or collections, writing a book does not seem to be the sort of process that can be readily crowdsourced.

However "Enterprise Social Technology" by Scott Klososky, published in early 2011, is a genuinely crowdsourced book. Even though Klososky appears to have an author credit, a closer look inside the book reveals that he is described as an "Aggregator" of the content.

Already working with a project manager and a publisher, Klososky started with outlines and notes of each chapter. The plan was then to crowdsource the writing of each section. The team posted the project on one service marketplace, but only got one response. After some input and tweaks to the proposal they placed the project on crowdSPRING and received 58 responses.

From this process 14 writers were selected from all over the world to write each chapter, based on Klososky's notes. This was considered successful, with each author adding extra content and insights. After two rounds of drafts the manuscript was complete. Each author is profiled at the back of the book.

The design of the jacket cover was also crowdsourced. 99designs was chosen as a platform and a contest organized to select the final design. This drew a very healthy 330 entries from which the 10 best were selected. The organizers then went through a further round of voting by asking peers, contacts, and social networks to select the best three of these. From this very final list, the core team picked the winning design.

Finally, the publicity was also crowdsourced. On the book website various bounties were offered for options for publicizing the book including:

- *five free copies if you reviewed a chapter on your blog (over 1,000 subscribers and at least 200 words),*
- *$50 to send an Amazon link to 2,000 social connections.*

It seems that some of this is tongue-in-check – for example $2,500 if you can persuade Michael Arrington or Robert Scoble to review it – and that there was in addition traditional PR activity.

However the result has been a crowdsourced book which has followed a traditional publishing model.

User testing

Crowdsourcing user testing involves using the crowd to test software or products to identify bugs, issues, and potential improvements before it is launched. Successful testing is a critical part of any software implementation project and crowdsourcing is emerging as a robust option.

> ## Benefits of crowdsourcing
>
> - Critical mass for software testing is important because the more bugs or user issues you identify the better your released product, so tapping hundreds of tech-savvy individuals can result in better outcomes.
>
> - Software testing is increasingly specialized with potentially many scenarios that need to be tested across platforms, devices, and languages. A global crowdsourced approach can cover this diversity.
>
> - There can be significant cost reductions, as the platforms provide access not only to experienced testers but also the communication and bug-tracking software required.
>
> - The testing phase of any software project is critically dependent on the preceding stages going smoothly. An "on-demand" testing model reduces the risk of paying an army of geeks to twiddle their thumbs for a week.

Example: uTest

The market leader for crowdsourced software testing is uTest, which claims to have over 40,000 registered testers on their books. The size of this pool provides depth in terms of global coverage, the type of applications that can be tested, and the kind of testing that can be done. Tests include functional, usability, and load/performance testing.

uTest seeks to add value by providing additional project management services as well as a platform to track bugs and facilitate communication. Its client base includes technology giants such as Google and Microsoft as well as much smaller businesses.

Other players

99tests, an Indian start-up that uses the mechanics of competition platforms and has the tagline "Meet the Bugs".

Mob4hire, a platform specifically for mobile application testing, specializing in usability.

UserTesting.com, providing on-demand usability testing on websites, sometimes as a one-off service.

Data analysis

The explosion of data creation over the last years means that many organizations have developed enormous databases of potential useful information. However data analysis is a complex and highly skilled task. Using crowds of data scientists to find the best ways of analyzing large data sets can be the most effective way of extracting value from those resources. It is also possible to break down data analysis into smaller tasks that can be performed by many people in a crowd.

Benefits of crowdsourcing

- Data mining and modelling is a specialist area, and few organizations have the in-house skills to do this well.

- Data scientists are often attracted to interesting real-world challenges and peer recognition as much as financial rewards.

- Data analysis and predictive modelling can be a highly creative domain, so getting broad input can allow the most relevant and novel approaches to emerge.

- In most cases the quality of predictive models can be quantified, providing unambiguous assessment of winners.

- Many businesses have very rich data sets that have not been subject to serious analysis, however sufficient budgets may have not been allocated and crowdsourcing can provide a lower-cost approach.

- There are also opportunities to partly crowdsource earlier parts of the process such as collating, re-formatting, or validating the data set.

Example: Kaggle

The most prominent data analysis platform is Australian-based Kaggle, which recently raised $11 million in funding. Kaggle uses the mechanics of a competition platform and sets up predictive modelling challenges for its crowd of data scientists, many of them academics. There are sometimes significant financial rewards, such as the $3 million Heritage Health Prize, however some competitions provide no monetary rewards, as data scientists are often motivated by other factors such as peer recognition.

Other players

In October 2006 Netflix offered a $1 million prize to whoever could improve their video recommendation algorithm by 10%. The final prize was awarded in October 2009 to a team which combined two of the previous top-performing teams.

Microtask platforms can be used to improve data quality and for some structured data analysis tasks.

Patent research

Patent research is an integral part of the process of both filing a patent and finding evidence to challenge one. In many instances companies need to find prior examples (or "prior art") of a patent's subject area. Crowdsourcing patent research to a wide community of patent professionals and amateurs has proved it can be a successful business model.

Benefits of crowdsourcing

- The more extensive the patent research the better, so a crowdsourced model, particularly if the community are patent specialists, can mean a deeper trawl to find previous examples.

- The intellectual property business is global and being able to get searches done by a diverse community based in many different countries is valuable.

- Being able to interact with a crowd during the process allows for unexpected avenues to be explored with directed searches.

- Using a structured platform allows companies who are dipping their toe in to the process to get advice on the necessary procedural steps to carry out the research.

- As in other instances, crowdsourced patent research can result in cost-savings compared to a more traditional route.

Example: Article One Partners

The dominant platform in crowdsourced patent research is Article One Partners. At present they do not have significant competition from crowdsourced patent platforms, only directly from traditional patent and intellectual property agencies.

The process begins when clients come to Article One Partners with a research request that provides all the relevant documentation. This is reviewed and scrutinized by the patent experts registered on the platform, who then seek examples of prior art, submitting evidence via the platform.

During the process clients can speak directly to the patent experts, which is important as this can help refine searches or give supplementary technical information. The researcher who comes up with the best examples can win up to $50,000 with smaller rewards for other active researchers.

Article One claims to have over 1 million registered researchers and to have distributed over $1 million in rewards.

Translation

Translation is an excellent application of crowdsourcing. The world is full of people ready to flex their multi-lingual skills for content that they care about. The quality of first-pass crowdsourced translations can sometimes be poor, however if translations continue to be improved and refined by others the output can become acceptable or sometimes very good.

> ### Benefits of crowdsourcing
>
> ■ Crowdsourcing translations is less expensive than using professional translators, though the quality is more variable, and it is better suited to non-specialist and non-technical material.
>
> ■ Using a global pool of potential translators can result in a faster turnaround time, with in some cases supply of translators exceeding demand.
>
> ■ Some crowdsourcing platforms have developed seamless technology to allow the easy delivery of websites and databases straight from a web interface to a community of translators.
>
> ■ In many cases translation quality will be poor so depending on the application you may need to add a professional review or crowdsourced check of meaning and grammar.

Example: Facebook Translations

One of the best known examples of crowdsourced translation is Facebook. In 2008 it launched a "Translations" app which delivered lines of text to be translated into different languages by Facebook users. To ensure quality, other users then voted on which was the best phrase.

This approach was so successful that a Spanish version of Facebook took just weeks to implement, and by the end of 2008 Facebook sought to patent the app. In 2009 they allowed websites that use Facebook Connect (for authentication using Facebook log-ins) to request a translation of their site using the tool.

Other players:

Lingotek provides a technology platform for community and crowdsourced translation which uses Facebook's approach of combining phrase translation and voting for the best options.

Smartling have a mixed approach using both a professional and crowdsourced translation to achieve high quality results.

Generalist service and microtask platforms such as oDesk, Elance, and Amazon Mechanical Turk all feature translation tasks.

Product design

Crowdsourcing product design through an entire life cycle from concept to finished product can draw on crowds in a variety of ways. There are a number of platforms that allow you to submit ideas, vote on the best ones, comment on and shape the design, and then finally buy the finished product, with a profit share going to the original designers and those who contributed.

> **Benefits of crowdsourcing**
> - Crowdsourcing product design can uncover interesting ideas, develop and improve them, and test whether they are commercially viable.
>
> - Crowdsourcing product design can significantly reduce risk if the number of pre-orders determines whether a design reaches the production line.
>
> - Interacting with the crowd creates a community of potential customers and brand ambassadors who may spread the word about your product, particularly if they feel a personal affinity with the creators.

Example: Quirky

Quirky provides a platform for what they term "Social Product Development." Registered users submit an idea for ten dollars and feedback is given by the rest of the Quirky community. Each week one idea is voted to be taken forward in the process.

The idea gets evaluated, shaped, moulded and tweaked by the crowd, with those making the best suggestions earning "Influencer" points. Finally the product is pre-sold on the website shop. If there are sufficient orders it gets manufactured. The inventor, the influencers who helped develop the product, and Quirky share the profits.

Quirky have taken crowdsourcing into the mainstream by selling their goods on U.S.-based home shopping channel HSN.

Other players

Japanese retailer MUJI has been an early adopter of crowdsourcing. It sources suggestions for new products from customers which are then voted upon, and given to professional designers to make into products.

Threadless invite T-shirt designs from the crowd, get them to vote on their favourite ones, and then produce them for sale.

Made.com is a British online furniture retailer where only the products that receive sufficient votes from customers are manufactured.

Consumer research

Consumer research provides fertile fields for crowdsourcing. The web has given a voice to consumer opinion and a crowdsourced approach provides an opportunity for brands to receive rich and valuable data to identify customer preferences, react to new products, and research their own reputation.

Benefits of crowdsourcing

- Crowdsourcing on a platform offers a structured way to get detailed, useful input from a broad range of consumers in a cost-effective manner.

- Aggregating the reactions and opinions of a large number of engaged people creates more reliable data and insights.

- Using an online method also means the data can usually be presented in real time to make analysis easier and allows questions to be tweaked to focus on emerging and unexpected trends.

- Crowdsourced consumer research can be more dynamic and interactive than traditional focus groups, leading to more valuable conversations.

- Connecting with a crowd can also help build a community of brand ambassadors and potential customers.

Examples: Crowdtap and Clickadvisor

Clickadvisor styles itself as an "online consumer research agency". It provides a platform to receive advice, innovate, and co-create with the crowd. Its approach is partly mediated as Clickadvisor.com itself invites "target consumers" to meet business needs.

Crowdtap offers a more self-service approach. Its consumers are usually recruited through social networks, and its platform offers a variety of tools such as polls and discussion boards to test consumer reactions. Users are profiled so clients can select and target particular communities. Crowdtap also says it engages and recruits influencers via social networks to help market brands.

Other players

Facebook has recently created a community called "Facebook Studio" for marketing agencies to encourage them to use Facebook for brand campaigns and customer dialogue.

Consumer research is also included in many individual company community sites, customer review platforms such as TripAdvisor, and websites that include product recommendations such as the Daily Grommet.

Search engine marketing

Search engine marketing (SEM) involves placing advertisements or paid links to appear alongside search engine results, based on the search terms entered by users. All major search engines offer search advertising, however significant research and analysis is required to select the most relevant keywords that will bring web traffic at a cost significantly below its value. Crowdsourcing can provide a very effective way of running SEM campaigns.

Benefits of crowdsourcing

- Effective SEM requires research and analysis, and small to medium businesses are unlikely to have the requisite in-house skills or resources.

- By using an crowd of experienced search engine marketers, campaigns can be created and rolled out quickly.

- Multiples perspectives and insights can uncover additional keywords or approaches that will benefit the client.

- Marketers can be rewarded based on their success, attracting the best and ensuring good return on investment for their clients.

Example: Trada

Trada created the SEM crowdsourced space with its launch in 2010. Its competition is still almost exclusively from traditional agencies. Trada has received funding of close to $6 million, notably from Google Ventures.

When clients come to Trada with a marketing campaign, Trada crowdsources the task to a crowd of experienced search experts (who they call "Optimizers") through their platform.

The Optimizers generate advertising copy, identify search keywords, and then monitor the results in order to refine the process. Optimizers earn a share of the value if they get clicks and conversions for less than the stated limit set by the advertisers.

Trada also provides advice for advertisers on how to frame their campaigns, a platform on which clients can see a summary of relevant data, and the opportunity to interact with the marketers who are working for them.

Social initiatives

The focus of this book is on using crowds commercially, however there are also many examples of the power of community being harnessed for social benefit. Of course connecting with crowds has always been a key part in charity and volunteering events. Crowdsourcing platforms provide new opportunities to reach out and help people in innovative ways.

Benefits of crowdsourcing

- Many people are keen to help and enjoy being able to contribute, often with minimal effort, through crowdsourcing mechanisms or platforms.

- Crowdsourcing platforms for social benefit allow individuals to see, be inspired by, and connect with a community of like-minded people.

- Crowdsourcing on mobile platforms can make it easier for people to contribute, and also often to reach those whose only digital connection is a basic mobile phone.

- Breaking assistance into smaller microtasks enables volunteers to help somebody immediately, allowing for spontaneity.

- The web knows no borders and can connect communities across the globe.

Example: VizWiz

One innovative example of crowdsourcing is VizWiz, an iPhone app aimed to aid blind and visually impaired people. If a blind person needs immediate assistance in identifying something they cannot see, they can take a picture with their iPhone and send a voice request for information. Members of the crowd then answer the request immediately, sending back a voice message through the app. The team behind the app have also used Amazon Mechanical Turk to source many of the helpers.

Other players

Most innovation and idea platforms also feature philanthropic and social challenges.

Samasource is a microtask platform designed to create opportunities for those in developing countries to earn a realistic living wage.

Ushahidi is a non-profit technology company which provides a quickly deployable open source crowdsourced platform for gathering data in crisis situations, for example in the Japan earthquake or Haiti.

Crowdrise adds a layer of crowdsourcing to individual fundraising pages.

PART VIII

CROWD BUSINESS MODELS

CROWD BUSINESS MODELS — VIII

USING OTHER PLATFORMS — VII

CROWDFUNDING — VI

MANAGING PROJECTS — V

USING SERVICE MARKETPLACES — IV

BUILDING RELATIONSHIPS — III

APPLICATIONS OF CROWDSOURCING — II

FUNDAMENTALS OF CROWDS — I

Crowd business models

The potential of tapping the power of crowds is rapidly becoming more apparent. While many businesses will see this simply as finding more effective and efficient ways to perform existing business functions, an increasing proportion of companies will start basing their core business model on crowds. This is leading to a wave of innovation in business, with outstanding opportunities for those that explore and populate this new frontier.

Chapter overview

- There are seven core crowd business models: marketplaces, platforms, crowd processes, content and product markets, media and data, crowd services, and crowd ventures.

- Each business models relies on a set of specific monetization models, including across transaction fees, subscriptions, and content and product sales.

- There are a range of success factors for the business models, which can be classed as contributor characteristics, buyer characteristics, and capabilities.

- Even though crowd business models can usually be rapidly scaled, there remain a number of constraints to that scalability.

Victors & Spoils: an advertising agency based on crowdsourcing

When it was launched in October 2009, Victors & Spoils was described as "the world's first creative ad agency built on crowdsourcing principles". Founded by three partners including CEO John Winsor, it has built considerable success, including creating campaigns for clients such as Harley-Davidson, Virgin America, GAP, and Levi's.

The company has close to 500 people from 126 countries in its contributor pool, all attracted through the firm's significant media and online visibility. Within this pool, it regularly interacts or works with around 200-300 of them, though none work predominantly for the firm at this stage.

The firm has built a reputation system to make it more efficient to find the best people for projects. Contributors are given points based on factors including how far their submissions go in the filtering process and client opinions, while creative directors can also allocate points based on their views of creative talent or collaboration capabilities.

One model they use is running an open brief, prepared by Victors & Spoils on the basis of the brief from the client. This is open to contributions from anyone. None of the submissions are visible to other contributors. In the initial round, contributions are ranked as A, B, or C. The client can then go through the submissions and choose the ones they want to pay for and use.

However the majority of the client work done uses what Winsor calls the 'pick and pay' model. Here, Victors & Spoils picks 10-25 people to contribute to the project, each of whom signs an NDA and is paid a small amount upfront for their submission. From this pool around 4-5 are selected to go into a further round, attracting additional payments. The company collaborates with these winners to further develop their ideas to meet the client's brief.

There are 12 people at the core of Victors & Spoils, including traditional agency roles of Creative Director and Strategy Director, as well as a Technical Director responsible for the platforms.

At the outset, fee levels for Victors & Spoils were around a quarter of traditional agency fees, but have risen to half to three-quarters of market rates. The partners started out with a 'better, faster, cheaper' philosophy, but now believe that the crowdsourced model often provides superior results to traditional agency models and so merits commensurate fees. In charging clients more, they can pay the crowd more and in turn attract better talent.

Crowd business models

There are many ways that crowds can help businesses achieve their objectives. For example, crowds can be tapped for a wide variety of critical services such as design, software development, advertising campaigns, or even product design.

However this often simply replaces existing approaches to sourcing suppliers or gets some of the organization's supporting functions performed in a different way. It does not fundamentally change the nature of the company.

Increasingly we are seeing entire business models that are fundamentally based on tapping contributions from crowds, where a primary source of value creation is from the crowd. In other cases companies are creating value by helping their clients use crowds well.

We are early in what will prove to be a long-term rise in the prominence and success of crowd business models. An increasing number of companies will shape themselves to create value using crowds. No doubt new crowd business models will emerge to complement the ones we can see today.

A taxonomy of crowd business models

Business models define how resources are brought together to create monetizable value. In crowd business models, the resources are primarily based on crowds. There are a limited number of structures in which the work of crowds can be monetized.

In the following pages we provide a framework that shows the seven primary crowd business models that aggregate crowd work to create value, and a description of the monetization and success factors for each of the business models.

Some of these crowd business models combine a wide variety of the crowdsourcing categories described in the Crowdsourcing Landscape shown in Chapter 1. For example Marketplaces covers service marketplaces, competition platforms, crowdfunding, and a number of other categories. The underlying business model for each of these categories is fundamentally the same, just applied in a different way.

We have also included Non-profit models in the Crowd Business Models diagram, so this can be fully mapped to the Crowdsourcing Landscape, however we do not cover Non-profit models in the analysis in this chapter.

Media and data

Creation of media, content, and data by crowds.

Knowledge sharing
Data
Content

Demand Media
Quora
Servio
Trend Hunter
We Are Hunted
IMDb
Data.com

Marketplace

Matching buyers and sellers of services and financing through mechanisms including bidding and competitions.

Service marketplaces
Competition markets
Crowdfunding
Equity crowdfunding
Microtasks
Innovation prizes
Innovation markets

Freelancer.com
99Designs
InnoCentive
Kickstarter
oDesk
Mechanical Turk

CROWD BUSINESS MODELS

Platform

Software and processes to run crowd works and crowd projects, for use with internal or external crowds.

Crowd platforms
Idea management
Prediction markets

Spigit
IdeaScale
Consensus Point
Napkin Labs
Kluster

Crowd services

Services that are delivered fully or partially by crowds.

Labor pools
Managed crowds

Ideas While You Sleep
BzzAgent
uTest
CrowdAdvisor
GeniusRocket
Victors & Spoils
Thinkspeed

Crowd ventures

Ventures that are predominantly driven by crowds, including idea selection, development, and commercialization.

Crowd ventures

MyFootballClub
my3P
SENSORICA
Globumbus

Crowd processes

Services that provide value-added processes or aggregation to existing crowds or marketplaces.

Crowd process

CrowdFlower
Data Discoverers
LiveOps
Scalable Workforce
Smartsheet

Content and product market

Sale of content or products that are created, developed, or selected by crowds

Content markets
Crowd design

Threadless
RedBubble
iStockphoto
Quirky
Beta Fashion
Made.com
RYZ

Non-profit

Citizen engagement
Contribution
Science

Kiva
Crowdrise
Ushahidi
FoldIt
OpenIDEO

Examples of crowd business models

There are many kinds of business models that draw on value created by crowds. Following are just a few examples that illustrate different aspects of crowd business models.

Data.com

Jigsaw Data Corp was acquired by Salesforce.com in April 2010 for $142 million and is now called Data.com. Its 2 million users pay annual subscription fees to submit, share, and access information on over 30 million business contacts. The crowdsourcing of contact information means that it is continually updated and validated, however Data.com now complements the crowdsourced data with information from Dun & Bradstreet and other vendors using more traditional data gathering and analysis models.

Demand Media

Demand Media's primary business is creating content that is monetized through search advertising. It draws on a stable of thousands of writers and video creators who are usually paid a fixed price per article, using sophisticated algorithms to request the content it believes will generate the highest revenue. It listed on New York Stock Exchange in January 2011 at a valuation of $1.3 billion, though its stock price has significantly declined since then.

Giffgaff

Giffgaff is a U.K.-based mobile phone service provider within the Telefonica O2 group. It claims "we're run by our members", with sales and support significantly performed by its users. Members who answer questions in the community space or generate sales to new users are rewarded with 'Payback' points that can be redeemed as cash, airtime credit, or donated to charity.

Kluster

Kluster began life as successful iPod accessories company Mophie but then pivoted into a crowdsourcing firm after it experienced at Macworld 2007 the power of asking its customers to contribute to its product development process. It now provides a crowd platform for clients to run their own crowdsourcing initiatives, and has also spun off ventures generated within Kluster, including the crowdsourced product design company Quirky, described in Chapter 24.

my3P

my3P is an online community created to help youth enterprise. Members earn points or potentially cash for performing tasks in the entrepreneurial process. This includes submitting ideas that earn points if others like them, doing specific tasks, managing projects, performing due diligence, and so on. The intention is that people get value from their contribution to a wide variety of entrepreneurial ventures. While my3P is not yet mature it points the way for business models that are entirely created and run by crowds.

Monetization

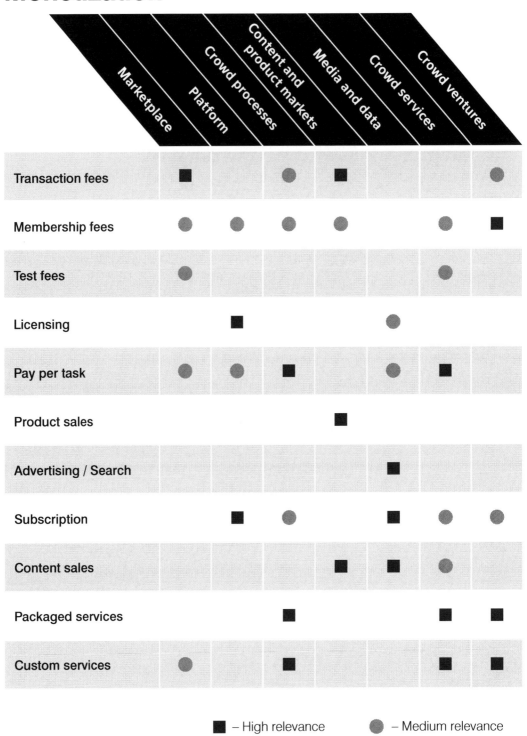

	Marketplace	Platform	Crowd processes	Content and product markets	Media and data	Crowd services	Crowd ventures
Transaction fees	■		●	■			●
Membership fees	●	●	●	●		●	■
Test fees	●					●	
Licensing			■		●		
Pay per task	●	●	■			●	■
Product sales				■			
Advertising / Search						■	
Subscription		■	●		■	●	●
Content sales				■	■	●	
Packaged services			■			■	■
Custom services	●		■			■	■

■ – High relevance   ● – Medium relevance

Monetization of crowd business models

Depending on the type of crowd business model, there are a variety of different approaches to monetization that can be applied. Below are brief descriptions of each of these mechanisms.

Transaction fees

These are especially applicable where crowd platforms are essentially acting as a broker between clients and service providers, in some cases aggregating the work created by the providers. Transaction-based payments can include job posting fees, bidding fees, and commission on payments.

Membership fees

Fees may be payable by either or both clients and service providers in order to participate in the platform, service, or value creation model.

Test fees

As tests are a significant aspect of how providers are assessed by potential clients, fees can be charged for taking tests on capabilities such as language abilities or software skills. Tests may be repeated by providers wishing to improve their scores.

Licensing

Software such as crowd platforms can be licensed for installations behind corporate firewalls. In some cases content including data can be licensed for re-use in a variety of formats.

Pay per task

Pricing may be based on particular well-defined tasks or services being performed for the client. In this case the margin received by the business is dependent on managing provider costs.

Product sales

Where products such as clothing, cards, gift items, or other goods are designed by crowds, the primary revenue source can be direct sales of those products.

Advertising

Revenue from content-based models can be generated primarily from advertising on the media generated. In some cases search advertising is the primary revenue source, in which case the content created needs to be generated specifically to maximize search visibility and user actions.

Subscription

A regular payment schedule can be established for either cloud-hosted software or for access to high-value content.

Success factors

	Marketplace	Platform	Crowd processes	Content and product markets	Media and data	Crowd services	Crowd ventures
Contributor breadth	■		●	■	●	■	●
Contributor quality	■			■	■	■	■
Buyer breadth	■	●	■	■	●	■	●
Buyer quality	■		●			■	●
Public reputation measures	■				■	●	
Internal reputation measures			■		■	■	■
Project management capabilities			■	■	●	■	■
Project management tools	■	■	■				
Content monetization model						■	
Quality control			■	●	■	■	●
Fulfilment					■		

■ – High relevance   ● – Medium relevance

Content sales
Packaged pieces of content such as books or reports can be sold in a variety of formats.

Packaged services
A clearly defined service at a fixed price can be delivered by crowds.

Custom services
Bespoke services can be delivered by crowds, with the company acting as an interface to the end-client through relationship management and quality control. This is significantly more complex than pricing packaged services, as fees need to be quoted and negotiated for each service, and it is rare to base pricing on labor costs.

Success factors: crowd business models
There are a variety of factors essential for success in implementing business models based on crowds.

Network effects
The challenge for these models is to develop both sides of these networks simultaneously, unless there is pre-existing pool from an established business. For example, design competition platform 99designs was established out of the existing deep pool of designers on SitePoint.com. This meant that with one side of the network established, only the client side of the market needed to be developed.

Contributor characteristics
Clearly crowd business models by their very nature depend on having many contributors. The two primary characteristics are the breadth and quality of the contributors, however not all business models require both.

Contributor breadth
In some cases having the largest possible pool of contributors is a fundamental enabler of a crowd business model. This can be attractive to buyers in marketplaces through the diversity of skills available, or in the scalability of access to those resources.

Contributor quality
Characteristics of high-quality contributors include domain expertise, keeping current in their field, excellent communication, offering creative solutions, and meeting deadlines.

Buyer characteristics
Contributors have substantial choices in the crowd ventures in which they participate. They will clearly be attracted to broad, deep pools of clients. However the quality of the clients is also

important. In the case of crowd services there is just one client, in which case its characteristics will attract – or not – the best providers.

Buyer breadth
In the case of models such as service and content marketplaces, a deep pool of clients is required to generate sufficient business for service providers.

Buyer quality
Clients that attract the most talented providers generally are sophisticated, offer interesting, challenging work, communicate well, have reasonable pay expectations, understand non-financial rewards, and respect the contributors. Where business models are based on crowd service delivery, a significant part of value creation comes from managing client relationships effectively, and thus attracting high quality and high value buyers. Specific skill sets that support success include defining objectives, pricing, managing expectations, and process communication.

Capabilities
There are a variety of capabilities that provide important foundations for crowd business models. Developing and sustaining these will be fundamental to success.

Public reputation measures
A key factor in attracting clients to marketplaces is having relevant and accurate reputation measures for providers, making it easy to find the most reliable, highest-quality providers. Contributors also find it valuable to see accurate reputation measures for the buyers, to maximize the chances of having a good experience.

Internal reputation measures
For crowd services and other models where the providers are not directly visible to end-clients, internal reputation scores that enable the identification of the best providers for particular tasks can provide competitive advantage. In a broader sense, being able to assess and select the most relevant providers for bounded talent pools is a critical skill. This usually requires effective use of interviews, internal tests, and trials.

Project management capabilities
Established project management processes and the ability to run these well is fundamental to any business model that requires service delivery by crowds.

Quality control
One of the most important yet challenging capabilities needed for many crowd business models is consistent and cost-effective quality control processes. In some cases these can be delegated to providers or crowds within strict processes to achieve maximum efficiency, however there are limits to this depending on the relevant quality criteria.

Project management tools

Clients often use marketplaces as much for the ability to manage projects and multiple providers easily as for the pool of talent they can access.

Content monetization model

While crowds can readily be used to generate content in a variety of formats, effective monetization models are required that link revenue including content sales, advertising, and search advertising with the specific content being created.

Fulfilment

For crowdsourced content and product markets, for example for articles such as art, clothes, or merchandise, competence at fulfilment including manufacturing and shipping is critical for success. While some companies outsource much of the fulfilment function, they still need to manage it effectively. Others find there is greater value creation in managing this process themselves, effectively making them crowd-fueled fulfilment companies.

Constraints on scalability

The beauty of business models based on crowds is that they are inherently scalable. If well designed, service delivery can be scaled extremely rapidly and broadly, while there are many ways in which revenue generation can be swiftly scaled.

However there are a number of potential constraints to scalability, even for crowd-based business models. Here are a few of the potential limits that need to be understood and managed effectively for rapid scaling.

Service delivery

Crowd-based service delivery provides massively greater scalability compared to services performed by in-house staff. However there are a range of constraints to doing this effectively.

Quality control

In general it is harder to achieve high quality standards using external providers, for a wide range of reasons including commitment, aligned incentives, degree of training, and so on. Increasing training and the degree of engagement with the company adds costs and slows additing contributors. Adding layers of quality control is usually essential, but also adds centralized costs.

The ability to create structured processes and layers of supervision in such a way that the quality control function can be largely performed externally is a key driver of scalability. It is a challenge that will be central to many emerging crowd business models.

Project management

As larger crowds are brought together into over-arching business processes, the effectiveness of project management structures can be severely tested. While extremely precise task definition and refined project processes can be scaled significantly, exceptions can rapidly increase. In addition, more creative processes usually cannot be put into overly tight project structures.

Availability of talent

In some cases for more specialist or highly creative skill sets, even crowds do not appear to yield a sufficiently deep pool of talent. This is most commonly a result of not being a good enough buyer in terms of rewarding contributors appropriately, including financially. However even where the business model can support and does flow through to adequate rewards to providers, attracting the right talent in sufficient quantities is not a given.

Revenue generation

Clearly the issue of scaling revenue generation is an issue for every business. However some of the challenges can be particularly pointed for a rapidly scaling crowd-based business model.

Defined offerings

Highly defined offerings are far easier to deliver using crowds, and can usually be marketed more effectively than customized solutions. Achieving precisely defined offerings, in some cases many distinct offerings to cater for a diverse market, requires a significant investment.

Evolving revenue sources

As markets evolve, existing offerings may lose traction and demand for new products or services may be recognized. This means that even well-oiled and highly-structured processes for bringing together crowd resources to deliver value to clients need to be continually changed and refined. The process of scaling can have many turns and forks in the road.

Getting results as a service provider

> " *Working online as a freelance provider is way cooler than working at a day job and I love it. In freelancing, you get to choose what things you want to do, how much you want to get paid and when you take a break.* "
>
> **Tamal Anwar**, Freelance blogger, Bangladesh

Becoming a provider on service marketplaces or other crowdsourcing platforms is rapidly growing in popularity in both developing and developed countries. As the practice enters the mainstream, the opportunity to make a successful living this way is becoming easier. As with starting any business it requires effort and commitment, but it can be interesting, challenging, and flexible. Specialists can earn good incomes, and it is possible to build significant companies by building teams of providers.

Chapter overview

- Starting out as an online service provider is challenging and requires persistence.

- At the outset it is critical to develop your online reputation through client feedback and building a portfolio.

- To win work you need to carefully choose your fees, sometimes bid frequently, and ensure you stand out in the bidding process.

- Competition platforms can provide opportunities for providers to win work, although it is difficult to make consistent revenue.

- Building relationships is the key to developing your business in the long term.

CASE
STUDY

Sakin Shrestha's story

Sakin Shrestha runs his highly successful software and web development business out of Nepal. In 2007 Shrestha started out as a solo developer, working freelance with a number of local clients. He specialized in HTML/CSS/PHP/Wordpress and used oDesk to bid for work. Wanting to expand, he decided to join an established company, Digital Max. The team was already on oDesk and as Shrestha knew the marketplace well it seemed to be a good fit.

He took the lead on oDesk and was able to significantly expand Digital Max's client base. Within 2 years Shrestha had taken the company's total working hours on oDesk from 500 to over 10,000.

In 2009, Shrestha decided he wanted to work on his own again. He already had some contacts, but also took various oDesk approved tests to help establish his resume and portfolio.

He comments, "It was a bit hard getting the first job. But if you try applying for jobs carefully after reading the requirements and address the specific questions then you will win the work."

Having established an excellent reputation and starting with his existing clients from oDesk, Shrestha started his own company, Catch Internet. Further building working hours, feedback, and ratings has allowed him to grow a global client base. Now the company no longer submit job applications, with all work coming from existing clients and invitations to be interviewed. The team recently clocked up 2,000 working hours.

The company now consists of Shrestha, four developers, two web designers, and two support function roles.

Shrestha's advice for success is:

- *Don't make fake promises*
- *Ensure good communication and time management with quick responses, fixed delivery dates, and effective task management*
- *Be online using various tools*
- *Try to build relationships to maintain and retain your clients*
- *Build a clean resume on oDesk using tests, a good portfolio, and great feedback*

Being a provider

Becoming a freelancer and growing your own business can be very rewarding. It can suit different working patterns and lifestyles and you can get a great sense of achievement by creating your own successful venture.

Service marketplaces can support developing this kind of business. At times the effort can be demanding – it requires a significant sustained commitment - but generally the best providers shine through and make it work. However it is important from the outset to recognize the challenges of setting up as an online freelancer.

Challenges for providers

CHALLENGE	COMMENTS
Establishing yourself	Real effort is required to start out, win work, and build your profile. Without visible experience and client feedback it is hard to win projects, although this gets much easier as you build up a portfolio.
Global competition	With a global talent pool you will be up against strong competition from around the world, with other providers sometimes offering low fees.
Home work	Freelancing isn't for everybody. It is challenging and can sometimes be lonely. You need to recognize whether your personality and working style is suited to work that will often be from home.
Technology support	To do your work you will need to have or have access to PCs, internet, software, and communication tools. You will need to organize your own technology support unless you can do it yourself.
Irregular work	Most work is project based so there can be times when there is either too little or too much work. This irregularity can be a logistical as well as a financial challenge.
Winning work	You have to keep on trying to win work which can be both exhilarating and frustrating. There is an ongoing cost in terms of time and effort.
Availability	If you are working with multiple clients they may demand things at different times, but you cannot always be available due to other work or family commitments. Be prepared that some clients will be unreasonable. The best approach is to be transparent about your availability and to try and build flexibility into your schedule.

Selecting the right marketplace

You should choose a service marketplace that suits your work and desired client profile. Often the best way to do this is to read about how each site works, find one that suits, and give it a try. If it doesn't seem right you can always try a different marketplace.

An overview of the most prominent service marketplaces can be found in Chapter 16. While the major marketplaces have many similarities, there are a number of factors that are worth considering in making your decision.

Charges

Service marketplaces make their money by taking a commission – usually somewhere between around 7% and 10% - on every job. Sometimes the cost is added on to whatever you bid so effectively is passed on to the employer, or is taken out of what you bid. Some marketplaces have subscriptions you can pay to lower the commission rate they take.

Receive payment

Payments are usually held using an escrow system so that money is held by the marketplace and then released when the project or milestones towards it are completed, though the process can vary slightly from site to site. Some marketplaces also have guaranteed payments for hourly jobs, usually if parties agree to use a monitoring tool which shows when a provider has logged in, and may take snapshots of their desktop. Finally many marketplaces allow flexibility in withdrawing money to a foreign bank, PayPal, or other facility. The cost and ease of doing this varies.

Helpful features

Each marketplace has a variety of features to assist both employers and providers, including monitoring tools, team rooms, and the ability to do video calls or share desktops. New features are being added all the time, and some can be very useful in supporting constructive client relationships.

Profile features

Check out what you are able to put on your profile. The more you are allowed to show, such as samples of previous work, the more chance you have of standing out from other providers. Some marketplaces also have their own approved tests covering basic skills (e.g communication) and specific project skills, which can be useful in demonstrating your capabilities.

Types of work

Some sites are focused on specific types of work such as programming, marketing, or writing. The bigger generalist marketplaces cover all these areas but some have a slight edge in particular types of work. Try out some searches on each platform to get a feel for how much of your target work comes up.

Reach

Some sites have a particular bias in their geographical reach, for example with more European or U.S.-based providers and employers. Most sites publish details of their user base and searching for work will also give you an indication.

Using multiple platforms

When you are starting out you should be wary about using multiple platforms. Although being on all the major platforms might sound like it gives you access to more work, it also potentially splits any client feedback you get. This makes it harder to build your online reputation.

Establishing online reputation

Before you are interviewed for a position, your feedback score and ratings are what employers will primarily rely on in selecting candidates. Initially you need to invest the time to create a great online profile and build up a portfolio of experience and client feedback. This is a prerequisite to success on service marketplaces.

Establish your online profile

Each marketplace allows you to create an online resumé that has several different features. Most of these are common across the different marketplaces. You need to spend time to get the wording of these perfect. If you are not writing it in your native language get a native speaker to make any corrections and make it sound natural.

Profile features

FEATURE	NOTES
Description	The main description of you and your capabilities should be succinct, but also needs to capture qualities that might make you stand out from others. Try to avoid clichés that are repeated on many others' profiles.
Categories	Marketplaces have standard categories for types of provider and sets of skills. Ensure you select the right ones to describe yourself so that employers can find you.
Education	Include details of any relevant degrees, qualifications, and certificates you have.
Job experience	As with a normal resumé, previous job experience can be important. Even though details of contracts won through the platform are available through your record, there is no harm in highlighting your contribution to major projects in more detail.

Continued on the next page >

Profile features (continued)	
FEATURE	NOTES
Tests	Most marketplaces have tests to demonstrate abilities in communication and language, and also specialist skills such as programming. These are definitely worth doing but only if you can do them well. You can attempt a test several times. If you are not a native speaker it's certainly worth doing the language tests, as many employers do go by these and some insist on them as a requirement.
Samples	Add samples of your work wherever possible.

Other web presence

To give a complete picture of yourself you should ensure that your broader online profile is visible and gives a strong impression.

Create an attractive, useful website. Ideally this will be provide the best possible showcase of your work and capabilities, so it can be a reference point for potential clients. Make sure any relevant social networks, particularly LinkedIn, are up to date and show you as an accomplished professional. You may choose to build a blog or Twitter account to become more visible. An increasing proportion of work requires at least some understanding of social media, so it can be useful to develop your skills in any case.

Getting great feedback

Excellent feedback is effectively a virtual currency on service marketplace sites. The best way to get it is to consistently do great work.

You should expect individual feedback on each job, and for your work record to be scrutinized. Individual ratings mean a lot, but the number of jobs you have done and range of work also point to your experience. Factors such as evidence of repeat work are important signals to potential clients.

To build positive feedback realistically you may need to start with a lower asking price to attract quality work, and use that to build a portfolio. It is quite acceptable to be up-front to employers about this, and there are many examples of how this strategy has lead to higher value relationships.

*I did not give up. Every week, I sent my applications to as many buyers as I
could. I made sure that my cover letter was impressive and outstanding.
I waited for a couple of months and a doctor from the United States hired
me as her virtual assistant and gave me a chance of building my reputation
on oDesk.*

Micah Lacsamana, SEO expert, Philippines

Winning work

Winning work is an ongoing activity for providers requiring constant effort. It has to be
considered as one of the built-in costs of your business. As you develop your reputation and
connections it gradually gets easier.

Pricing strategies

The best employers consider quality of work to be more important than fee levels in selecting
providers. However pricing too high, or even too low, relative to others providing similar
services can put off potential clients. You need to carefully consider fee levels.

Set your rate

When you're starting out look through provider profiles and job specifications to see the rates
that are being offered. Do not set your fee too low. It has to be something that you can live
on and also a reflection of what you are worth. Fee levels can stay the same with repeat work
for some clients, so be aware that even if you raise your fees you may still be doing some
work at your original rate.

Fixed vs hourly fees

There will be opportunities to pitch for both types of assignment, and some providers prefer
one model to another. Generally hourly rates are much less risky, particularly for longer
projects where the overall time required is unpredictable. If you are very experienced at a
particular type of work fixed fees can potentially be more profitable, but that is subject both
to unexpected challenges in doing the work, and the client changing the scope.

Consider value in quoting fees

Consider how valuable a job is to you personally, and take that into account in the fees you
quote. In some cases, such as where the work is guaranteed or ongoing or where there are
considerable non-financial benefits (such as building up feedback or establishing an important
relationship) it is worth offering a lower price.

Lowballing was annoying, but I was diligent and the phase didn't last long. Because the competition was so intense on Elance, good feedback was crucial and I had to lowball just to land a contract. Looking back on it, I consider it an overhead.

US-based freelance web editor

Bidding

Bidding for work is one of the challenges of becoming a provider. It can be repetitive and time-consuming, but doing it well gives you an edge over other providers.

Frequency of bidding

Realistically you will have to submit many bids to win work, particularly when you are starting out. A 5% rate of winning bids or even less is not uncommon.

Know when to put in effort

A major issue is that generally the more directed and specific your bid is, the more likely you are to win it. But these are the bids that take the most time.

If there is a job that has real long term value (either leading to more work or because it offers non-financial benefits) then put in extra effort. Similarly spend more time if there is work which is a perfect fit with your skill set and you feel you are more likely to win.

Check out feedback

Before bidding, always look at previous feedback about an employer from other providers. You want to make sure they are a reasonable person to work for and that they are a good match with the way you work. Also see how they have rated other providers. If they frequently give low ratings it may be better to avoid them.

Stand out from other providers

Being a provider is competitive. To successfully win work you need to differentiate yourself from other candidates.

How to stand out	
Do trial tasks	Trial tasks are commonly used by employers either to identify the best provider or to validate the selection of a candidate. Be prepared to do trial tasks as you can expect to get paid, usually the task is quite short and you will also get a feel for what working for the employer is like. It reduces risk for both sides.
Go the extra mile	You can stand out by giving more than is required during the job application process. This may be through contributing ideas, doing a small sample of the work, or demonstrating you really understand what the client is looking for. Time constraints mean this approach needs to be reserved for the jobs you really want to win.
Cover letter	Spend time on the cover letter as it is the best way to differentiate yourself prior to the interview stage. If you want to win the work, you must customize the message, demonstrate that you understand what is being asked for, and address all the specific points or questions asked in the job description.
Interview confidently	Interviews can be voice or by text. These are not only a place to sell yourself but also to see how you might get on with the employer. Make sure you are honest on your capabilities and availability. Being realistic is more likely to win work than lose it.

Using competition platforms

Competition platforms are an option for providers but they are certainly not for everybody. It tends to be much harder to make money from competitions than on service marketplaces. With a high risk of not being paid many freelancers do not regard them as a viable option.

Competition range

There are a wide variety of competitions. Competition platforms tend to be subject specific, focusing on work such as graphic design, writing, or data analysis. The mechanics and process of these contests are similar, however the rewards can vary from less than $100 for a simple logo competition to in some cases over $1 million for innovation competitions.

Reasons to enter

Make money	Making decent money can be viable on some of the more lucrative competitions particularly if you have a highly specialist skill, but only a handful of people are able to make consistently good income from competition platforms.
Gain experience	Competitions can provide experience and useful lessons in the work process and interacting with clients.
Build profile	Winning a contest can be useful for building your profile, and make you visible to clients.
Use the output again	If you enter contests and don't win you can use the output in other situations, sometimes with a little tweaking. In almost all cases you own the copyright on entries that don't win.

Winning strategies

The quality of your work relative to that of the competition is the most important driver of creating a winning entry. However there are other factors, not least the client's style and views. There are a few principles that can help make the most out of competition platforms.

Choose your minimum price

Decide on the minimum fee you require to enter a competition, however be aware that the higher the fee, the more competitive it becomes.

Refine based on feedback

The best competitions allow you to interact with the client and view their interaction with others. This gives a clear indication on what they want so you can refine your entries to suit. Gain insights from entries the clients have said they liked, but never copy them.

Enter mid-competition

It can be best to wait until you see client feedback before submitting any entry. You can then enter knowing what the client likes.

Developing your business

Once you have established yourself and have a critical mass of clients and feedback ratings you can consider how best to grow your business.

Build repeat clients

Where possible develop long-term relationships with your best clients. There can be real effort in putting in the effort to demonstrate your value, however also recognize that you can save significant time and effort in avoiding continually bidding for new work.

Build complementary teams

It is useful to build relationships with other providers who have skills that are complementary to yours. This can allow you to do work together and bid for work you could not do on your own.

Be transparent

You may go from being one person to working as part of a team or sub-contracting work to others. Always be transparent with your clients about who is doing work and the arrangements you have.

Avoid scope creep

Scope creep occurs when projects are not scoped correctly or are badly project managed. They end up being delivered late and accruing extra hours which in fixed fee situations are usually not recoverable. Often this will be the fault of employers who do not know what they want. Developing your business successfully means avoiding scope creep. Avoid projects where clients are not clear on what they want, insist on milestone payments upfront, or suggest a scoping phase prior to the full project proceeding.

Establish networks

Even if you don't build up teams you may be able to refer work to other providers when you do not have availability or they have different skills. Developing networks of referrers can be a powerful source of new business.

Similarly your clients will have networks that you may be able to get work from if you have a particularly strong relationship.

From provider to employer

It is a big step to go from being a solo freelancer to building what is essentially a professional services company. While some have rapidly grown large businesses, recognize that there are many challenges to doing this successfully. Hiring and retaining quality workers is increasingly difficult, not least because they always have the alternative of working as individuals.

The biggest potential draw for workers is consistent work, so if you are able to generate a steady flow of work, price it well, and manage projects efficiently then you have the starting foundations for growing a successful online services business.

Go to the book's companion website

www.resultsfromcrowds.com

For:

- Additional resources

- Crowdsourcing landscape diagram and examples

- Crowd business models diagram

- List of crowdsourcing services

- Updated information

...and to provide feedback and input for the next edition of *Getting Results From Crowds!*

Made in the USA
Charleston, SC
12 October 2012